FROM FURY TO FREEDOM

Raul Ries
with
Lela Gilbert

HARVEST HOUSE PUBLISHERS
Eugene, Oregon 97402

The names of certain persons and places mentioned in this book have been changed in order to protect the privacy of the individuals involved.

Special thanks to Lela Gilbert
for taking the torn memories of my past
along with my life today and putting them
together in this book. I pray that
it will be used to bring many to know
my Lord and Savior Jesus Christ.

FROM FURY TO FREEDOM

Copyright © 1986 by Harvest House Publishers
Eugene, Oregon 97402

Library of Congress Catalog Card Number 85-082383
ISBN 0-89081-537-2

To Sharon, my wife, who prayed for me
faithfully all these years.
To my sons: Raul, Shane, and Ryan
whom God gave me through His love.
I pray that this book will be strength
to your lives and a blessing by changing
the lives of those who read it.

FOREWORD

In reading the life story of Raul Ries, I was moved to know how much God protected this man and his family, and dealt with the family abuse. *From Fury to Freedom* is a positive book that will encourage many families to admit some of the most private, even intimate and depressing feelings they have had to endure. The realization that God is the ultimate answer for all their needs will help them to live through these devastating dark days.

We cannot deny that our God is a God of miracles. He took Raul from the pits of hell, from the cocoon of despair, insecurity, fear, hate, and self-destruction, into the most wonderful healing—SALVATION; the healing of his soul and spirit. Raul is evidence of how God's grace can spare the life of a young boy and nurture him into manhood. Jesus cradled Raul's head in His bosom, and kissed away his pain. He gave him the direction and love for which he was desperately searching.

I'm so happy that Raul is now living for Jesus—what a tremendous miracle! God has brought Raul, his sweet red-haired wife, Sharon, and their children into the knowledge of what Christianity is all about; the transformation into a beautiful, godly family.

I have known Raul a long time. He is one of the greatest teachers of our time. He is marvelous! His knowledge of the Bible is truly a gift from God. His present congregation at Calvary Chapel in West Covina, California, is evidence of his excellent pastoral abilities. I am amazed at the wisdom and love of this man. Raul Ries is an inspiration and has the aroma of success. This book shows the two kinds of love—the human love and the Divine Love. When these two elements get together, something supernatural and exciting happens in a person's life.

My prayer is that this book will be an ointment of healing for many devastated families and individuals. Will you, please, enter into the exciting drama of—*From Fury to Freedom!*

NICKY CRUZ
Evangelist/author
Colorado Springs, Colorado

One of the great proofs of the validity of Christianity is the radical changes for good it makes in one's life. The Greek philosophers denied the possibility of redemption. They declared that once a man was down, there was no recovery. The life story of Raul Ries stands as a proof of the power of Jesus Christ today to redeem the lost and thus shows the Greek philosophers to be wrong.

It has been my joy to see the transformation of Raul's life as the result of his conversion. So much love now emanates from his warm smile it is hard to believe that his life was once so filled with hatred that killing brought him joy.

His story reads like that of a modern day Saul. A man who once destroyed is now being used mightily by God to build the kingdom.

CHUCK SMITH
Senior pastor
Calvary Chapel of Costa Mesa

CONTENTS

1

Mamacita's Prayer

My sports car turned into the driveway, street lights gleaming back at me from the carefully waxed red hood. I grinned to myself as I opened the garage door. A sweetly seductive smile was warming my thoughts. One of my better-looking kung fu pupils had caught my eye several times that night. There was a tempting invitation in her eyes when she said "Good night." And on the piece of paper she had softly closed into my hand was a neatly printed phone number.

Feeling handsome and cocky, I walked briskly to the front door and rang the bell. No answer. My spirits sagged. *Sharon knows I don't have my housekey. Why does she go off and leave me locked out?*

Then I remembered—it was Sunday night. Bitter thoughts clogged my mind. *She's at church. Of course! Little Miss Christian.*

I walked around the house to the backyard, slamming the gate in frustration. Once again I would have to break into the house through the kitchen window. As I stepped around a couple of battered trash cans I made an outrageous discovery. My expensive, nearly new exercise weights were in the trash! *Why, that _____!* *I'll teach her to mess around with my stuff!* I slammed my fist into my open palm.

Panther, our faithful German shepherd, cautiously licked my fingers as I stood, paralyzed with rage, staring at the discarded weights. "Hi, Panther. Hi, baby. You hungry? Didn't she feed you?"

I glanced around the backyard, irritated by the sight of innumerable dog piles. "She just won't clean up the yard for you, will she, baby?" Again fury gripped me. It wasn't that my wife hated Panther; she just wanted *me* to clean up " . . . so the kids can play back there, Raul."

"Clean it up yourself!" I'd yelled at her. "I've got a job. I'm going to college. And I run a kung fu studio. All *you* do is sit around the house or go to church."

I climbed through the window, as I'd done so many times before. Sharon was always annoyed because I didn't carry a housekey. "Why do you make me drop whatever I'm doing and run to the door?" she would ask. "What's so difficult about putting a key in your pocket?"

"Big deal. You're never doing anything anyway!" I'd snap. "You've got nothing *better* to do than let me in my house."

I swung open the kitchen door, headed for the living room, and nearly tripped over something in the hall. Suddenly I froze in my tracks. *Suitcases!*

So she thinks she's really going to leave me! Sharon had threatened to leave a thousand times, but this was something else again. My eyes raced frantically around the room. A hole in the wall exactly the size of my fist caught my attention. "Please fix it, Raul!" she had pleaded. "I don't want to have to explain it to my folks."

"_____ your folks!" I had spat out the words, shoving her out of my way. "You make such a big deal out of everything!"

Now I collapsed in my chair, trying to collect my thoughts. Conflicting emotions of burning hate and a strange sadness confused me. Photographs of our boys' smiling faces stared at me: Little Raul; Shane. Sharon would take them with her. In my imagination I could see Sharon happily married—to some stranger. I could see my sons calling someone else "Daddy." Tears stung my eyes momentarily. *Why couldn't it be us? Why was there no peace in our home?*

But those tender feelings quickly vanished in my swelling rage. I could feel the all-too-familiar hardness as I shouted at the silence, "So you think you're gonna leave me? Well, just maybe you're wrong, lady! If I can't have my family, nobody else is gonna have them either!"

I jumped to my feet, charged across the room, and yanked open the closet door. Fumbling in the darkness and frantically pushing heavy garments out of the way, my fingers finally closed around the object of my search—the smooth, icy barrel of a .22-caliber rifle. I pulled it out and examined it. Then I groped around the closet shelf for the shells. Grimly and expertly I loaded the weapon.

"I learned a few things in Vietnam, lady. Killing ain't so tough."

I sat down in the chair again and balanced the rifle across my knees. Within seconds I was back on my feet, restlessly pacing. A car door exploded the quiet. Anger and fear swirled inside me. I waited. Nothing. Must have been next door.

I sat. Stood up. Paced. Flipped on the TV. Sat down. Watched. Listened. Listened some more.

That night didn't end the way I had planned. No one, least of all Raul Ries, could have guessed the amazing twist and new direction my life was about to take. But what had brought me to such desperation in the first place? What could cause a man to plot the death of his wife and sons? I had lived 24 years consumed by hate, anger, and violence. Why? Where did it start? How did it grow?

• • •

I can still see myself—a thin, big-eyed child trapped in the shadows of the Mexico City night. Although I was no more than five years old, I had waited in the chill time after time.

Each day followed a similar pattern. In the morning my father would take me with him to his job. Throughout banking hours I would keep busy around the stone building where he worked. Time passed pleasantly as the interesting parade of people coming and going fascinated me. But by afternoon I began to feel dread. Soon the financial district would lock its big, dignified doors, and my ordeal would begin.

After work I would straddle the back of Father's motorbike as he wound his way through the busy streets to his favorite nightclub. There his "other" life captivated him. Father always left me at a newsstand just outside the club entrance. I could smell the liquor and see bluish clouds of smoke drifting through the partly opened door. "Wait here!" he would sternly command.

Time dragged. Eventually one kind woman or another would bring me something to eat—a plate of beans and rice with a few strips of overcooked meat. I would wash it all down with lukewarm Coca Cola. And I would wait.

I was bored, frustrated, and sad. Many hours passed. Many people came and went—a far different array of characters from the ones I had watched earlier that day at the bank.

At long last Father would emerge. He would be drunk—and dangerous. He would roughly plant me on his motorbike and we would take off on the dizzying ride back home. Mother would be waiting for us at the door. "You worthless drunk!" she would yell. "You've spent every extra cent on your _____ whiskey!" Father would slap her face and push her toward the bedroom. His curses, her screams, and the sound of blows would fill the house.

How I hated my father! And to me, Mother was just about as bad in her own manipulative way. Still, I naively believed that Mother needed my protection. Perhaps that's why my younger brother, Xavier, and I would often find ourselves embroiled in the violence. Our household continually reeled with emotional outbursts.

Fortunately for me, there was one haven. I called my grandmother "Mamacita"—little mother. She was the only one who seemed to really love me. In terror I would flee from my father's fierce anger and race across the city streets to Mamacita's beautiful house. I would enter the elegant courtyard of her home, lush with plants and hidden from the city noise. Instantly my tense young frame would relax.

"Welcome, Raul! I'm so glad to see you!" she would greet me, her black eyes sparkling with pleasure. "Do you want to stay tonight?"

"*Yes*, Mamacita! I'd love to stay!" I wondered if she knew I was avoiding a whipping.

"*Good!* We'll rent some bicycles tomorrow. You and Sonia can ride together!"

"Thank you, Mamacita!" Before I could catch my breath she would bring me food on my favorite plate, along with a glass of cold, creamy milk.

Mamacita's home reflected more wealth than ours. She worked night and day in order to keep financially afloat. Her hands were seldom idle. When she wasn't serving customers at her little grocery shop, she was knitting clothes to sell. My father's drinking precluded any luxuries in our family. Still, our apartment was clean. We had food to eat. We were not poverty-stricken.

The real contrast between our homes was not economic. Mamacita's home had a peace about it. I could be "at home" there, without fear of poisoned words or punishment. While Father and Mother's vile language ripped into my soul, Grandmother Ries spoke softly and there was love in her eyes.

Apart from Mamacita's home, peace was an unfamiliar sensation. From my earliest years I longed for it. Yet the more I sought peace, the more it eluded me; it was always driven away by my own inner turmoil.

There were times when I couldn't even take refuge in Mamacita's home. One afternoon when I was about seven years old, Mamacita was staying at our apartment. I got into an argument with Xavier, which was not unusual. We were more comfortable exchanging blows than compliments. Unfortunately, this particular time my father was home. He tried to separate the two of us in our frantic clawing and clumsy punching. When we continued to battle, his impatience led to violence. First Father grabbed Xavier by the neck and tossed him across the room. Then he headed for me. "I'll kill you, you no-good drunk!" I yelled, the words spilling out of my young heart before I could stop them.

"Why you little _____!" His language was harsh, but the fist that split my lower lip was brutal. Hot blood coursed down my chin. Then he picked me up, carried me to my room, threw me into bed, and locked the door from the outside. "Don't you get up, or I'll teach you *another* lesson!" he yelled through the door.

It was no later than 4:30. The sun would burn in the hot summer sky for several more hours. I lay silently in my bed, blotting my mouth, too proud to cry. The hours crawled. I couldn't escape to Mamacita's house—she was here with us. I had no choice but to lie there and wait until sleep caught up with me.

Finally the city grew quiet as darkness brought relief from the heat. I dozed, my face throbbing where my father's fist had left its purple marks. I awoke to the sound of a familiar voice. Mamacita was in the hallway outside my room, walking quietly and praying softly. I could hear her voice shake with stifled tears: ". . . and Father in heaven, I pray for my grandson Raul. I pray for his protection. I pray that he will grow to be a strong man, a healthy man, a man who will know God. And I pray that he will find peace. Father in heaven, let there be peace around him. And let there be peace within him."

An inexpressible longing stirred inside me. But when I tried to pray too, no words came. I began to sob in the lonely silence.

Mamacita had prayed for me. . . Mamacita always prayed. I wondered if anyone ever answered her prayers. Was there really anyone named Father-in-heaven? Was He anything like Father-in-the-room-across-the-hall? Finally I fell into an exhausted sleep, undisturbed by dreams, peaceful or otherwise.

Three more violent years awaited me, years in which Mamacita's prayers seemed unheard and unanswered. By the time I was ten years old, life was intolerable. We had moved to an adobe house with a dirt floor. Sometimes we didn't have food. Our lives were threatened on a daily basis by Father's increasingly violent rages. No escape seemed possible. Even in Mamacita's faithful smile, the light of hope seemed to have dimmed. What would become of our battered family? Would anything ever change?

2

An Unexpected Journey

It was a chilly autumn morning in my tenth year. I awoke to unfamiliar stirrings in our little house. Rubbing my sleepy eyes, I tried to identify the noises that had interrupted my sleep.

Drawers were opening and closing. Clothes hangers were being moved along the closet rods. Was that a suitcase snapping shut? My eyes opened more widely, and I stared at the ceiling, trying to think of what might happen today.

All I could remember was the argument I had heard the night before, a fight that had begun just as I was dozing off. Of course it wasn't unusual for me to hear my parents screaming at each other, but last night's quarrel was somehow different. My mother had sounded more sure of herself, and less vulnerable. Father, in all his drunkenness, was whining and pleading instead of threatening.

And now all this activity—what was going on? Before I could get out of bed to investigate, the mystery was partially solved. ''Raul! Get up and get dressed! We're

going on a trip!" My mother's voice was sharp with
urgency. "Get dressed *now!*"

"Going where?"

At least for the moment, my question was unanswered. But my heart began to pound with excitement.
A trip! And Father was nowhere around. I hadn't heard
his voice once. Could we possibly be going somewhere
without him?

Hope lifted me from my little bed and led me to my
clothes. Almost instantly Mother was there, helping me
dress quickly. She hurriedly packed the rest of my
belongings in a tattered overnight case.

Within minutes I found myself scrubbed, combed,
and wearing my very best shirt and pants. "*Where* are
we going?" I repeated the question breathlessly as
Xavier, Sonia, and I followed our mother to my uncle's
waiting car.

"We're going to the airport." My mother spoke
calmly and with quiet pride. "We are going to fly to
Tijuana, and then drive to the United States of America.
We are leaving your father!" All three of us children
cheered spontaneously. Our young eyes had seen
enough drunkenness, enough beatings, enough fighting
to last the rest of our lifetimes. The wind that morning
was crisp with fall, but sheer joy warmed me to my
toes as we made our way to the Mexico City airport.
Plastic seats faced the terminal windows, and we could
watch the big airplanes taxi on and off the runways.
I was almost speechless with anticipation. This was a
new beginning. Already the clouds of depression and
dread that shrouded my everyday life were beginning
to clear. No more fear!

In my entire life I had never lived a day apart from
the shadow of my father's wrath. Even when I was at
Mamacita's home, the time was always just ahead

when I would have to return to our hate-filled household. What would it be like to be free?

The sound of the airplanes and the bustle of the rushing passengers added to my exhilaration. Soon our flight was announced. We headed for the gate to board the plane. I silently said goodbye to Mexico, with my only tinge of sadness that I was leaving Mamacita. But surely I would see her again. Today the world was mine!

The flight itself was a marvelous adventure for a child my age. Xavier and I were caught up in the wonder of soaring above the clouds. When we landed in Tijuana, we were greeted by an entourage of smiling strangers. I quickly learned that they were my aunt and uncle—my mother's sister and her husband.

Piling into their shiny, late-model car, we children were wide-eyed and mute. As if the plane ride hadn't been thrilling enough, we were about to drive to Los Angeles—in the United States of America! But first there was a stop at the boarder. Uniformed men examined our suitcases and asked for papers. Finally we were allowed to pass through.

All of our lives America had represented hopes and dreams, and the ultimate escape from dissatisfaction. Now it was our home. What would it be like? we wondered. Would we have a big house? What did the food taste like? Would we make new friends?

These questions turned in our minds throughout the drive. But their importance was overruled by one immense understanding: Father would not be here. That would make up for any new experience that might intimidate other children. For us, nothing was frightening —except *him*.

My uncle drove slowly toward the house at Third Street and Huntley Drive, allowing us to quietly absorb the sight. It was large and handsome, with neatly curtained windows and well-swept sidewalks. Grandma and Grandpa Fernandez, my mother's parents, rented this lovely place. And within its carefully painted walls was the same peace and love I had first experienced in Mamacita's house.

Grandma's eyes were wet with tears of love at the sight of us. And Grandpa was my *friend*—I knew it the first time we met. "You kids just wait!" he said; "we're going to take you *everywhere*! Have you heard about Disneyland? We'll go there. And to Knott's Berry Farm—it's just like an old-time Western town! And when it gets hot again, we'll go to the beach. You're going to love it here!"

And love it we did. Our whirlwind exploration of Southern California's fabulous attractions went on for months. To the eyes of everyone else, we probably looked like another carful of happy tourists. But to us, it was more. We lived in an environment rich with laughter, affection, and compliments. It was a place to grow—to thrive.

The next fall I started Catholic school. I was in the third grade, and I knew absolutely no English. I watched the nuns who taught us communicate easily with everyone else, and it was almost funny being totally unable to understand. Fortunately, play is a universal language for children, and my quick smile found me friends in the schoolyard. Soon I began to make sense of the new words and inflections that filled my ears.

Within months I spoke enough English to survive. And as I sat day after day in that devoutly Catholic environment, learning catechism as well as writing and arithmetic, I wondered, *Could I ever be a priest? I might like that.*

On Sunday I served as an altar boy. My impressionable young mind responded with fascination to the sacred traditions—the candles, the statues, the processions and chants and robes.

While I was an acolyte, I often thought of Mamacita. Her form of worship was different. She never prayed to the little statues. Apparently she wasn't interested in all the rituals and rites. Sometimes she would use her rosary beads, but she never repeated the usual "Hail Marys" or the Stations of the Cross. She just prayed to her "Father in heaven" for her family. I was intrigued by the thought that maybe Mamacita and all these religous people knew something I didn't. Maybe Someone in heaven did answer prayers. Sometimes I'd look at the crucifix above the altar and feel a tug inside. Was it my imagination, or was there some power there, drawing me to...but what? I did not understand.

Meanwhile, during our happy months in America my mother received letters from my father, and she always answered them. Seeing Father's handwriting stirred up an uncomfortable feeling in the pit of my stomach. Still, he was far away. What harm could a few letters do?

But one evening, after an especially delicious dinner prepared by my aunt, Mother matter-of-factly informed me, "Father is going to meet us in Tijuana next Saturday."

"For a visit?" I hadn't seen him for so long that a visit didn't seem too bad.

"Well...yes. A visit." Mother's eyes looked sad and distant for a moment. "Yes. He's coming to visit us." She flashed a feeble smile to hide her feelings.

Something in her expression sent a chill down my

spine. *This wasn't right.* The pained look on Mother's face disturbed me deeply. Surely she didn't miss *Father!* Surely she wasn't thinking of...the idea was too upsetting to imagine.

The first time we drove to Tijuana to see Father, I rejected his awkward attempts to embrace me. I coldly answered his questions but kept my distance. To me it seemed absurd that Mother would ever want to see the man. I was too young to comprehend any desirable attraction between the two of them.

Before long we were meeting Father every weekend. "I don't *want* to go!" I snapped at Mother one morning when she told me we were about to make the three-hour drive. "I *hate* him!"

"Well, you'd better get over *that!* I've almost finished getting his immigration papers together. Next month he will be coming here to live with us."

Tears burned in my eyes. I wanted desperately to run—somewhere, anywhere. "Are you *crazy?* How could you do this to me? He'll just start beating us all up again!"

"Raul, your father has *promised* me that he won't drink anymore. He says everything is going to be different now. And I really think he means it!"

"Oh, yeah? Listen. He'll *never* change! I'll never stop hating him. And I'll never stop hating you for making me live with him again!"

It was impossible to express or even understand the tidal wave of emotions that washed over me after that conversation. I had learned to treasure the simple pleasure of tranquility. Intuitively I knew that the peacefulness within our new home was about to vanish.

Father arrived in the spring of 1959 and got a job at the Bank of America where Mother worked nights in data processing. Our family took over the downstairs rooms in the big house on Third and Huntley Drive. Before long those rooms were cluttered and dirty, for Mother slept during the day while Father worked. No one did housework.

But worse than the disorder was the disconcerting tension I felt the moment I walked through the front door. Gone were the smiling greetings from Grandma, the hugs from my aunt, the friendly tousling of my hair by Grandpa Fernandez.

Father's promise to stop drinking didn't last long. Within weeks he was coming home drunk, and he and Mother were fighting just as frequently as they had in Mexico City. That brought quick words of hate and defiance from me, and Father responded by wielding his hand against my stiff, skinny body. I often prayed that my dad would die and leave us alone.

My hatred for Dad fostered open hostility with my mother. I hated her for allowing Dad to return to our family, and she would react to my angry words by telling me that I was dumb and stupid and would never amount to anything. It didn't help that my brother Xavier was considered a genius and seemed to always receive Mom's praise.

One evening Father made an unexpected announcement to the family: "I've found us a house," he said proudly. "A house of our own!"

"Where is it?" Mother looked interested and hopeful.

"A man I know at work says he'll rent us a place in Montebello."

Within weeks the little world I had built around myself in Los Angeles was a thing of the past. We moved to a new home and made new friends. I left the Catholic school and entered public school. And life was more difficult than ever. This unfamiliar place, away from loving relatives, was full of violence and anger.

To add to the chaos, another baby entered the family
. . .my sister Chris. My young spirit began to burn with
rage. Sports was my only pleasure: I lived to play baseball, to compete in track and field, to challenge my
friends in flag football. And when I wasn't playing a
sport, I was staring at one game or another on television. Watching the worst team in town was better than
trying to get along with my family.

My fanciful dreams of the priesthood had completely
vanished. I continued to attend church on Sundays just
to avoid another hassle in the family. But I could not
understand how the priests could conduct mass, then
go out and drink and smoke. They didn't seem any
holier than anyone else. Church seemed like a meaningless ritual. If God even existed—and I was beginning
to have serious doubts about that—then why didn't He
answer my prayers about Dad?

After four turbulent years in Montebello, we moved
again. This time my parents bought a home in Baldwin
Park. Now that I was approaching adolescence, my own
emotions were more volatile than ever. Two things appealed to me: escape from my violent family and somehow expressing the anger that raged within me. There
was one soft spot left in me that belonged to a German
shepherd dog given to me when he was six months old.
Dad didn't mind the dog, but Mom hated him and
threatened to give him away. I named the dog "Panther," and every night after school I'd spend an hour
or more training him. Those moments together were
my only escape from the unending turmoil at home.

My first year at Balwin Park High School was marked
by an increasing number of unpleasant episodes: fights,
trouble in class, and days of ditching school. Finally,
at the age of 15, I decided that life in America was no
longer for me. Father's return had shattered all my

hopes and dreams. Hate ruled my spirit. There was only one place I could go where someone loved me, where Father could not be found. That thought alone kept me from losing all hope.

I would bide my time, wait for the right moment. Then I would return to Mexico City and find my way to Mamacita. And I would go alone.

3

Escape Across The Border

"Panther!" I shouted as I ran gleefully toward our house, glad to have ended another schoolday. "Panther! Come here!" Normally my canine friend bounded out of our yard to greet me. But today he was nowhere to be seen.

I flew through the front door, dumping my notebook on the nearest available chair. "Panther...where are you?"

"Panther's not here right now," my mother snapped as she came into the room.

I felt a jolt of fear. "Where is he?" I demanded.

"Well...he's...somewhere special today. You can see him some other day."

"Mom! Where is Panther?" Now I was panicky. "Did he get hurt?"

"No, Panther's fine. Don't worry about it." She started to leave the room. I trailed her persistently.

"But, *Mom*..."

Sonia came in from outside. "Did you tell him?"

"Tell me what? What's going on?"

"Mom gave Panther away. Didn't she tell you?"

"Oh, no! Mom! You didn't really do that!" I was stunned. This had to be a joke. I coldly stared at my mother and asked, "Did you, Mom? Did you?"

"That lazy dog! All he does is make a mess."

A smile seemed to play around the corners of Mother's mouth. Was she enjoying my pain? "I should have gotten rid of him a long time ago!"

"I don't *believe* this!" I shouted. "I just don't believe it! Mom! I love Panther! How could you do this to me?"

"What's done is done!"

"But—"

"Shut up, Raul!"

I stormed into my bedroom and slammed the door. My eyes were swimming with tears, my mind flooded with disbelief and shock. The never-ending dispute between my mother and I had escalated into all-out war the past few months. Father's explosions punctuated our family life with unpleasant incidents. But my mother's words constantly tore at me with what seemed like never-ending criticism and correction. While Father drank and raged, Mother worked to undermine everyone else's relationship with him. It was as if she hoped to win his approval by finding fault with us children. And as the most belligerent of all, I was unquestionably her number one target.

In my young eyes, my parents were impossible to love in the best of circumstances. Still, this incident with Panther was unprecedented in its coldness. Mom knew how much I cared about Panther—knew it very well. As far as I was concerned she had hard-heartedly set about to hurt me. And she had succeeded.

Sadness, however, was not my prevailing reaction to the loss of my dog. As the hours passed in the solitude of my room, I became more and more outraged. Life was intolerable—it had been so for years. I could not and would not exist in these circumstances any longer. The time had come! That night, while my family slept, I plotted my course.

Next morning the clatter of breakfast dishes marked

the beginning of another schoolday. I stared blankly into my bowl of cereal, moving a spoon automatically into my mouth. My mind was obsessed with the knowledge that this was my last meal in this wretched house.

As Sonia, Xavier, and Chris left for school, I swung my leg across my bike and headed down the street toward Baldwin Park High School. But school was not my destination.

With bitter determination I made my way past El Monte Boulevard, past Rosemead, toward the eastern edge of the Los Angeles City limits. It was a warm, clear morning and I began to relax a little as I pedaled with steady rhythm toward my first goal.

I rode past the rapidly deteriorating buildings in downtown L.A., past the winos, past the sleazy bars. They made only one impression on me: I knew that by the time I hit skid row, I would be just blocks from the Greyhound bus station. Then I would catch a bus to San Ysidro, and from there it was only a few steps across the border into Mexico.

When I reached the busy bus terminal, I looked over the throngs of people and tried to locate the ticket window. There it was, just inside the building! Nervously I left my bike as close to the door as possible and scurried inside.

"How much does it cost to go to San Ysidro?" My words were spoken calmly, hiding the fear that fluttered within me.

"Five dollars, son." The kindly man gave me a curious look.

"Thanks," I mumbled and tore out the door. Walking my bike up and down the sidewalk, I eyed the pedestrians who passed me. Impulsively I approached a prosperous-looking man. "Sir? Want to buy my bike?" I was embarrassed to hear a crack in my voice as I spoke. "Five dollars!"

The man looked at me, then at the bike. It was a nearly new ten-speed in mint condition.

"Five dollars? Are you sure?"

"*Five*. I've got to catch a bus."

He pulled a crisp bill off a bulging money roll. "Sold, kid!" He wheeled my bike toward a nearby car, turned a key to open his trunk, and chuckled to himself. I rushed back toward the ticket window.

"A ticket to San Ysidro." I stated coolly, avoiding the man's questioning eye. Without a word he put the five-dollar bill in his register. A bright blue ticket slid out of the metal counter. I grasped the paper prize in my hand as if it were purest gold. Within an hour I was sitting in a smoky bus, headed south on the San Diego Freeway.

About the time I began to enjoy the ride, we disembarked. The Mexican border was just steps away. I caught up with a mother and her two children and walked past the border into Tijuana, looking very much like a fourth member of the family.

Phase one was completed. Now I faced the most challenging task of all. How would I get from Tijuana to Mexico City? For a moment I wished I had tried to sell my bike for ten dollars. But there wasn't time to feel sorry about my empty pockets. I quickly located the Three Star bus station. "Which one goes to Mexico City?" I asked a busy-looking man. He pointed to a rickety vehicle just across the street. I ran toward it and grabbed the driver by the arm.

"You've got to help me!"

He stared at me and frowned. "What are you talking about?"

"I've *got* to get to Mexico City. I'm running away from my father. He hates me and I *have* to reach my grandmother's before he finds me. I've got to get there *fast!*"

The driver hesitated. He started to shake his head, then noticed the enormous pile of baggage that he would soon have to load into his bus. "Well...all right. All right! I'll tell you what. You load the bus and I'll take you along."

My best smile flashed across my face. Sincere gratitude swelled in me. "Thank you, sir. Thank you!"

After hurriedly stowing the cargo in the bus's ample belly, I found a seat right behind the driver. Together we watched the road ahead as he carefully maneuvered through the crazy city traffic and on into the countryside. "I'm Jorge," said the driver as we hit the open highway. "What's your name?"

"Raul. Raul Ries. Hey, I really appreciate your help."

"I'm not supposed to do this," he said sternly. But I noticed a hint of a smile as he glanced at me in the rearview mirror. "You don't live in Tijuana, do you?"

"No. I lived in Los Angeles. But I'll never go back there."

Tentatively he asked me about my father, my family, my running away. I told him all my frustrations, and as the miles and hours went by the stories grew more and more detailed and exaggerated. Before long my alcohol-tormented father had become a total madman who beat me daily with a board. Despite my exaggerations, the driver seemed to believe me.

He started to ask me about my grandmother: "Who is it you're going to live with then? Your father's mother, or..." His sentence was never completed. A swaybacked horse grazing along the side of the road stupidly stepped into our path.

We swerved, but it was too late. There was a loud thump as our bus screeched, then careened wildly and nearly turned over. People screamed in terror. We finally came to a stop and everyone fought to get out quickly. The threat of fire was very real.

The mangled animal lay dead by the roadside. Our bus was mortally wounded too, its weary engine hopelessly damaged by the impact.

At this point Jorge, the bus driver, became my guardian and protector. In nearby Guadalajara he had me stay with him in his hotel room while the company arranged to send another bus. The next couple of days we wandered around town. Jorge bought my meals. At night he would find a female companion and leave me alone in the hotel room while he enjoyed some adult entertainment.

Finally, after three days, the replacement bus arrived and we completed our journey to Mexico City. At the terminal, Jorge stuffed some money in my hand, put me in a taxi, and gave the driver instructions.

Soon I was confidently striding up Mamacita's driveway. I rang the bell, then jovially hid behind a hedge. When she opened the door, I jumped out with a shout: "Surprise!"

Mamacita was most assuredly surprised. I had been missing for nearly a week. My parents had informed her, and, like the rest of my family, she was worried.

"I want to live with you!" I blurted out. My story spilled out without eloquence or skill. "I *hate* my parents. I hate living in America. I want to stay here and never go back."

Mamacita fed me, listened to me, and calmed me. Quietly she told me about how her husband had died when my father was a little boy. "Your father had a lot of responsibility," she said. "He had to help bring up the family."

"But why does he get drunk all the time, Grandma?"

"I know, Raul. He's been drinking since he was a boy. It's his way to escape from the pressure for awhile. But, Raul, he loves you..."

"If he loves me, why does he beat me? He's always blaming me for everything. And Mom's always putting me down."

"Raul, you need to be more understanding. Your parents do the best they can. But they have a lot of pressure."

"Well, I hate them and I'm never going back. I'm going to live with you."

"You can't do that. You have to go back and love them."

"I'll never love them."

"Raul, I want you to call your parents and tell them where you are. They'll be so relieved to hear you're all right."

It was a couple of days before I called, and Dad was surprisingly calm. He said he would be down in a few days to talk to me and bring me home. "Don't bother!" I told him. "I don't ever want to see you again."

For the next week I settled into the peace of Mamacita's home. I had almost forgotten how quiet life could be. In her loving way she tried to help me see how good God was, and that He had His hand on me. I listened, wanting to believe that what she said was true. But my life, and the hurt my grandma had endured, confused me. God couldn't care about us and let us suffer, I thought.

Finally Dad arrived. I greeted him coldly, expecting threats and hateful words. But for once he surprised me. He tried to reason with me, to change my mind with promises.

"Your mother's sorry about Panther, Raul. I talked

to her about it. She says she'll quit hassling you if you'll just come back."

"I hate her, Dad! I'm not going back."

"Look, Raul, try to understand. Your mother has problems. We all have problems."

"I won't go back."

"You have to go back."

"No I don't! I'm staying here."

When Dad couldn't make any progress, my grandmother tried again. "Raul, you must go back. You can't live with me. Try to understand and forgive your parents. They really do love you."

Then Dad promised, "When we get home, everything will change." I wanted to believe him; I had to believe him. But the next day as we headed for the bus station, I knew nothing would change. When Dad asked me to carry our bags to the taxi, I told him to carry them himself. And so the battle of wills began. During the long three-day bus ride back to Tijuana, we fought constantly. No matter what he said, I disagreed. If he told me to do something, I rebelled, knowing he couldn't beat me with all the people around.

At night I stared out the bus window at the clear, starfilled sky and thought about the brief moment of freedom I had enjoyed. I recognized that nothing would change at home, and I began to think of only one thing—escape. Not a temporary move to Mamacita's. I could hardly wait until I turned 18 years old so I could leave home for good. Could that possibly happen sooner? "God," I prayed, "help me escape!" Over and over I prayed that prayer. But as we drew closer to the border, I sensed the futility of that prayer. God didn't care about my problems. If I wanted to escape, I would have to find my own way. If necessary, I would fight for it.

4

The Young Warrior

I slipped into my jeans, popped a blue T-shirt over my head, and grabbed my ever-present black leather jacket. One of my P.E. buddies yelled, "Hey, Raul, where've you been the last week?"

"I was away on *business*," I answered with a quick smile and a sweep of the hand. "You know how it is." Several guys in the locker room laughed at my characteristic bravado. Actually I'd been suspended from school again. I had lost track of how many times that had happened over the past three-plus years.

I sauntered over to the mirror to comb my hair and discovered that one of the bigger guys was hogging it, taking his time to make sure every lock was in place. After peering between his arms a couple of times to let him know I was waiting, I informed him, "You know, it ain't going to get any prettier."

The guy, a lineman on the jayvee football team, slowly turned to face me. "You got a problem?"

"Yeah, you! You're in my way."

I stiffened as he grabbed the lapels of my jacket. "You

36

got a long wait, pal, cause I ain't in no hurry.''

The locker room was instantly quiet, for I had a well-earned reputation as a troublemaker and street fighter. I stared at him for a moment, then with a flick of my forearms knocked his hands off my jacket. Immediately I aimed a shot at his throat. Backing him into a corner, I landed a flurry of punches to his face and watched him crumple to the floor.

My friend Tom pulled me away before I could do any more damage and led me out into the hall. "Guess I showed him," I said. Tom laughed. He was my best buddy and accompanied me on most of my adventures.

After my return from Mexico, I had asked myself a thousand times why I had listened to my father and Mamacita. Predictably, life did not improve at our house. Hopelessness haunted me. Once my efforts to escape from my parents were foiled, I settled for an alternative that helped vent the pent-up rage I couldn't express at home. Every week I found my way into more confrontations, more fistfights, more violent displays of anger. The hate I was unable to fully exhibit at home was turned toward strangers, young men who "asked for it." Usually they got more than their fair share of my wrath.

On the Baldwin Park High School campus, my humor and cheerful smile brought me friends, popularity, and plenty of female attention. Despite the rumors, only my closest friends, like Tom, knew both sides of my personality. Besides, the fact that I never showed up hurt must have made me seem like a fairly respectable person. As we walked toward my locker, I felt cocky. Once again I'd proved who was really tough.

Tom's girlfriend, Barbara, lockered next to me. As we approached my locker, I noticed again the pretty senior girl who shared Barbara's locker. We had kidded each other a few times between classes, and I had noticed a peacefulness in her personality that seemed irresistible. I had a girlfriend at Edgewood High, but this lively redhead frequently caught my attention. "Hey, Tom! That chick there—what's her name?"

"The blonde?"

"No, the redhead. She shares Barbara's locker. What's her name?"

"Oh, that's Sharon. She's got a boyfriend, man."

"Hey, I'm not interested in *that*. I just wondered what her name was—that's all."

Sharon, I thought to myself. She had a certain quality that made me want to know her better. *That's a pretty name. I'll have to remember it next time I talk to her. Sharon. She seems like a nice girl.*

Halfway through my next class I was ordered to report to the principal's office. The guy I'd punished and the P.E. coach had reported my actions. "It wasn't my fault," I told Mr. Gilbert.

"It's never your fault!" The principal was trying to control his voice and not yell as he stood over me. "You're in dozens of fights and it's never your fault. It's always someone else's fault. You expect me to believe that?"

"No."

"You're a danger to the students of this high school. Every time I walk outside there's a kid with a busted nose or a broken face complaining about you. I've got to protect my students from guys like you. You're a menace to society."

Mr. Gilbert walked back behind his desk, made a quick notation on a pad, then curtly informed me, "You're suspended for two days."

This was my second suspension of my senior year. But as I walked out into the cool, foggy air that was typical of fall mornings in the San Gabriel Valley, I laughed, thinking of the fun I could make during my "vacation."

The days were taken up with my new hobby, kung fu. My love of sports, particularly baseball, had continued through high school. Secretly I dreamed of playing major league baseball. But I also enjoyed fighting. The manager of the supermarket where I worked that summer had suggested I go with him to learn kung fu. This was the ultimate discipline that incorporated all of the martial arts. The kung fu expert could use his hands, feet, and other weapons to become a complete fighting machine.

Nights were spent with Tom and my other buddies in the Hessians. We were a car club, sponsored by the local police, that provided our favorite burger place with some of its most faithful customers. Every Friday and Saturday night a dozen or so of us gathered there to eat—and to wait for some action. If it didn't come to us, we went looking for it. There were always parties to crash, and often they were the scenes of violent confrontations. When Raul Ries arrived at a party, everyone knew that a fight would soon break up the event. We Hessians thought this was great fun. A little alcohol and a few well-placed blows made our night.

This particular weekend the action found us at our burger hangout. On Saturday night a car full of Mexican "cholos" drove up. We Hessians were popular, "cool" guys, and we looked down on these "greasers." Our folded arms and smart remarks stated our position all too well. One of the Mexicans was a huge, overweight character. He didn't like my looks or my comments, and obviously he hadn't heard about my reputation. He aggressively walked up to me, glared at me, and kicked my car. Rage immediately engulfed me. As I moved menacingly toward him I yelled, "What's your trip, sucker?"

He responded with a swinging right. That's all it took. I flew at the unsuspecting assailant like a whirling tornado, fists and feet flying. My intention was not to caution him or to stop him; I wanted to hurt him—badly. Of course, we weren't the only ones involved, as our fight prompted a full-scale brawl between my car club friends and the other Mexicans.

I rarely got hurt in these situations. I was so violent that no one could get near me. As usual, I lost all control and before long the pudgy challenger was lying flat on the pavement. Yet for me that wasn't a signal to stop. I kicked him repeatedly until I could see blood oozing from his body.

"Raul! Are you crazy?" Tom tried to pull me away. "That's enough. . .you'll kill him." But in my demented state I kept on blindly kicking—in the head, in the groin, in the side. The fat boy's groans gratified me. I felt pleasure at the sight of his bleeding.

Now Tom seriously interceded. "Come *on,* man. The cops will be here any minute. Let's split." Two other Hessians helped Tom pull me away. We all started cracking up at the sight of the fallen giant who lay heaving at our feet. Most of his buddies had already split, having seen enough of my rage. We jumped into our cars to make our escape, but too late. Two police cars with revolving red and blue lights stopped us cold.

"Ries! What happened this time?" the officer in charge demanded. Though the cops knew me and liked me, they tired of the frequent complaints about my activities.

"These guys came from nowhere!" I explained. "They started the whole thing. You should have seen them. They started hassling us, kicking our cars, hitting us. We were just defending ourselves, officer.''

My smile and open arms seemed to convince the weary policeman that there was at least some truth to my story. "All right, get out of here," the cop ordered. "And stay out of trouble. You understand?"

"Oh, yes, sir," I smiled with total insincerity. Not only could I fight my way out of just about any problem, but I could lie my way out too. My glib tongue had saved me from jail so many times that it had become a joke among my close friends.

Monday morning I was back in school, and as usual I was late. Scurrying around a corner for my first-period class, I bumped into Sharon. "Sorry! You okay?"

"Oh, hi, Raul!" Was it my imagination, or had Sharon's eyes brightened a little when she recognized me? She quickly asked, "How was your weekend? What did you do?" Her pretty smile framed the innocent question.

"Me?" My mind raced. There was no way I would tell this prospective female admirer what I *really* did on the weekend. "I just went to a party with some friends. You know." The first bell had already rung, so this was no time for small talk. "Hey—got to run. See you around?"

" 'Bye, Raul. See you.''

I tried to catch my breath as I settled into my desk. As the teacher began to drone on about the lesson, I couldn't help but review the events of the previous weekend. *Women never understand fights*, I thought. *Sure, they like strong, brave guys, but they don't like the fights that produce the heroes.*

To tell the truth, I didn't feel the least bit guilty or remorseful for any of the pain I caused. In fact, I felt wonderful during fights, and afterward I felt like a glorious victor. Fighting was an ideal outlet for my hate and bitterness. I rarely knew any of the guys I beat up. As far as I was concerned, they existed only as "statistics."

There was another reason why I couldn't let the girls know what went on during our weekend escapades: Other females were involved. These were easygoing one-nighters who were glad to please us and never hear from us again. Those habits would seem senseless to most of the girls we knew.

I did have a girlfriend—Terri, who went to Edgewood High. But we only went out occasionally, for steady dating would have interfered with my weekend fights. Terri was okay. But Sharon . . . she was a completely different kind of girl. In fact, she was starting to look very attractive.

At lunch hour Sharon shyly walked up to me. "Raul?" She flashed her beautiful smile and I was all ears. "I have to ask you something."

"Sure! Ask me *anything!*" I spread my hands in a display of mock generosity, and she laughed.

"I don't know if you've heard . . ." Her shy voice grew a little more confident. ". . . I've been selected as one of the homecoming princesses."

"Oh, hey! Congratulations! You'll be the cutest one there!"

Sharon flushed at my compliment and continued. "I'm dating a guy that already graduated from high school. But I can't take him to the dance because I have to go with someone from here."

"Oh, yeah?"

"So, I was wondering if . . . maybe . . . you'd be my escort at the homecoming dance?"

"No kidding?" I felt proud and happy about this new

opportunity. "I'd love to take you there. Tell me when it is."

"A week from Friday night. After the football game."

"Thanks for asking, Sharon. I'd really enjoy that."

After we made further arrangements, we parted and went to our afternoon classes. This gave me a new sense of importance—being invited to escort a homecoming princess. Of course, I'd have to miss my Friday-night carousing, but this was worth it.

There was one element that made me nervous, though. Tom had told me that Sharon's parents were some sort of missionaries. They called themselves "Christians." Devout Catholics I knew that I could handle, but I wasn't too sure about religious Protestants.

On the big night I was on my best behavior. Sharon's mother greeted me at the door. "Hello. You must be Raul! It's so nice to meet you. Please come in!" Sharon's father welcomed me with a warm handshake. I was a little surprised by their friendliness. Were these people for real? I wasn't quite sure what they expected from me, so I couldn't really play the game.

It was a relief when Sharon appeared and we said goodbye. She looked absolutely beautiful in her simple peach-colored dress, and her specially made-up hair complimented her pretty face. "Have a wonderful time, you two," her mother said as we left. "See you about midnight."

We went to the football game and I watched as the princesses were driven around the field at half-time. Then we attended the dance. Sharon wasn't like any girl I had ever taken out before. She wasn't cheap—or easy. And she acted like she was really interested in me. Of course, I was very interested in her. So I told her only what I thought she needed to hear.

After I took Sharon home that night, I drove away thinking about her. She had a quality that I longed for. But what exactly was it? Her home? Her smile? Her style of conversation? Whatever it was, she left me wanting more.

Mamacita's face flashed into my mind, then vanished. Just a coincidence, I thought. Surely Sharon and Mamacita had nothing in common.

I drove past the burger place on my way home. Nothing was happening. Mildly disappointed, I turned down my street and parked outside my home. This had certainly been an unusual Friday night. In fact, I was surprised that the usual fury within me was subdued; I didn't really miss the weekend rumble. I sat for a moment in my car before heading into the darkened house. *I'll have to take Sharon out again*, I concluded.

5

Beating The System

Sharon and I didn't start dating immediately after that memorable homecoming evening. But lockering next to her allowed for frequent contact with plenty of friendly kidding. It was obvious that my nocturnal activities would not mesh with her background, so I didn't push for a relationship. Still, I thought about her more than I intended.

I also thought about baseball. I was excited about my last varsity season at Baldwin Park High School, and maybe later playing professionally. But that dream was crushed when the coach kicked me and my friend, Ed, off the team for fighting. We pleaded with him to let us back, but he was tired of our disruptive attitudes. I couldn't believe that the coach would destroy my future career because of a little fight. That further intensified my anger, which was vented in more fights.

Later that spring a friend called one evening. "Hey Raul..." he whispered urgently into the phone. "I'm at Alcala's party. Your girl, Terri, she's here with another guy...some little rat from Edgewood. Just thought you'd want to know."

I was infuriated. It didn't matter that we'd dated infrequently in recent weeks. I had asked her out that night. She had told me some relatives were visiting and she couldn't go anywhere. What a slap in the face!

"That two-faced _____!" I cursed as I jumped into my car and peeled off into the night. My first stop was at Tom's place. "Let's get all the guys together. We're going to teach that _____ to mess around with my chick." We drove to the burger place and picked up three or four Hessians. We picked up five or six more at Bob's. By the time we arrived at the party, we were a dozen strong. Two girls screamed when they saw us coming. A quiet foursome slunk away into the darkness, knowing all too well what lay ahead. We marched in with ready fists—and we used them.

The brawl lasted a long time. The young man who had made the mistake of taking Terri to the party felt my full fury. He gained firsthand experience in my expert kicking techniques. He got a close-up of both my fists. Once I started, I was so enraged that I couldn't stop. I wanted to kill him, and I nearly did.

When we finally left, my victim was unconscious on the floor. My friends were less amused than usual, but I felt terrific. I had made my point more forcefully than ever. We drove off to relive it over hamburgers.

Tom acted worried as we ate. He tried to laugh as he said, "Man, you really did a number on that sucker."

"I know," I cracked up. "He won't be taking Terri home tonight!"

Tom just rolled his eyes. "Right...not tonight."

Of course, I knew that Terri and I were finished, but that didn't matter. Now I could concentrate on

Sharon. But it turned out that I had bigger things to worry about than my romantic notions. The following Tuesday, during math class, a homely girl marched in and handed the teacher a note. "Raul Ries. Please report to the principal immediately."

"Now what?" I sighed. I hadn't done anything disruptive in school for days. With a loud, bored groan I strutted off to the school office.

The principal's stern face was, of course, very familiar to me. The two scowling men with him were not. They remained grim as Mr. Gilbert introduced us. Then one of them spoke. "Raul Ries, you are under arrest for assault and battery. You have a right to remain silent. Anything you say may be used as evidence against you...." Of course I had heard the Miranda warning plenty of times on television, but incredibly, despite countless fights and scores of injuries inflicted on other people, this was my first arrest.

The two plain-clothed policemen handcuffed me and escorted me to their car. At the West Covina Police Station I was fingerprinted and booked. Bail was set, my parents were notified, and I was ordered to appear in court a week later. Tom met me as I left the courtroom. "I guess my number came up," I told him with a weak grin.

The fight that finally put me in the hands of the law was the one caused by Terri's "unfaithfulness." The Edgewood student who had taken her to the party was in critical condition when the paramedics arrived. Everyone knew I was the one who had beat him up.

We met again in court. His cold stare—I didn't bother to remember his name—greeted me as I entered the drab room. But even then I felt a stirring of pride as I looked at him and noticed several scars from our encounter. I had overpowered him in combat, and in my mind he was forever a loser.

There was no doubt about my guilt, and my court-appointed lawyer advised me to plead guilty. The only question was whether I would spend one or two years in jail.

As I stood for sentencing, I received a surprise. The judge stared for a long time at his file before looking at me. "Raul Ries, you have pled guilty to the crime of assault, causing serious bodily injury. The court has given a lot of thought to what would be best for you and for society. The court has decided that if you want to serve your country in the Marine Corps, sentence will be suspended and you will be allowed to do so."

I couldn't believe my ears. I had escaped again! I had two friends in the Marines, and they had both wound up in Hawaii. The decision was obvious: "I'll enlist in the Marine Corps, your honor," I politely replied.

I almost laughed out loud as I saw my victim limp dejectedly away with his family. *I beat him again,* I thought as I left the courthouse with a cocky smirk on my face. *Ries, you've got this world licked.*

There were only a few weeks left in school before graduation, and I made sure I kept a low profile. The highlight of that period was the all-night senior party on Catalina Island. Sharon also went, and we ended up spending most of the time together. "What are your plans after graduation?" I asked.

"I'm planning to attend college. I'll probably start at junior college, but I hope to transfer to a Christian university. After college I'm thinking about going to Chile to live."

"How come?"

"I grew up there. My parents were missionaries to Chile and Colombia, and that's where I've lived most of my life. What are your plans, Raul?''

"I'm enlisting in the Marines!''

"Really! How impressive.''

"Yeah. I go to boot camp next month. And then I'll probably be assigned to Hawaii.''

"Will you write to me?'' Sharon asked.

"Sure, I'd love to.''

For the next four weeks before I headed to Camp Pendleton, Sharon and I spent a lot of time together. The more I was with her, the more I wanted to be with her. In her presence, the rage that normally controlled my life lost its power. She gave me reason to start a new life. With her encouragement I could leave my problems behind, go into the Marines, and return home a hero.

Part of that new Raul meant attending Sharon's church. I had attended church for most of my life, but it had become meaningless ritual. What difference did it make whether I attended the Catholic church or Sharon's church? If she wanted me to go with her, that just meant more time that we could be together. Still, it was an adjustment.

The church she went to in Baldwin Park was a simple stucco structure. It looked sterile, and the inside was totally weird. The first time I attended, I wondered why there were no statues or candles. And what about stained-glass windows or a huge cross with a gruesome depiction of the crucifixion? How about the organ with pipes protruding from the walls? Instead of an ornate altar in front, there was a small table with a large Bible on top.

There was no procession of priests wearing vestments and parading behind altar boys carrying a cross or swinging a pot of incense. Instead, several men in plain suits walked onto the platform. One of them led the congregation in some plain-sounding hymns. Another coordinated the offering. Then a third opened his Bible and began to preach. By the middle of his lengthy sermon I had fallen asleep.

That first Sunday Sharon was polite, but obviously disappointed. We went to lunch with her parents, and afterward I hopefully asked, "You want to go out next week?" No girl could ever resist my casual invitations.

"I don't know, Raul. I'll see."

Next time stay awake in church, stupid, I lectured myself sternly after dropping Sharon off at home.

The next weekend, Tom arranged a double date for us with Barbara and Sharon. We escorted them to a party at a friend's house. As much as I enjoyed Sharon, some of my old habits were hard to break. Half an hour after we arrived, Tom and I went to a back room and did some heavy drinking and fooled around with some easygoing chicks. An hour later we returned to the party to discover that Sharon and Barbara had left without us.

I knew I'd blown it. Sunday morning as I scowled at myself in the bathroom mirror, I determined that I would need to do something to try to salvage the relationship. Sharon and I were certainly getting off to a rocky start, and most of it was my fault. Okay, all of it was my fault. I dropped my arms and took one more look at my hair. Not bad. I shrugged off my romantic anxieties. "Don't worry, babe," I promised myself, "she still digs you."

After church, Sharon sweetly inquired about my disappearance. "Tom and I were trying to help Ron," I said with my best smile. The party was held at Ron's house, and Sharon knew that his family had a lot of problems. "You know, Ron's old man's really been getting on his case. Hey, how come you left early?"

"Barbara wanted to leave. I'm sorry."

"Hey, no big deal. How about a movie tonight?"

And so I survived another rocky situation with my charming smile and quick-thinking explanations. Since I didn't have much money, most of our dates were movies or else watching television at Sharon's home.

One month after graduation I reported for basic training at Camp Pendleton, outside San Diego. Immediately I wondered if I had gotten myself into something worse than jail. As we scrambled off the bus, a sergeant yelled at us, "Move! Move! Move!" Quickly we lined up for our first instructions. "You're no longer in the outside world!" the sergeant yelled. "From now on you do what I say. You don't look around. You don't open your mouths unless you're told to speak. You keep your eyes to the front at all times. The first word that comes out of your mouth if you're told to say anything is 'Sir.' 'Sir, yes, sir.' 'Sir, no, sir.' And so on. Do you understand me."

"Sir, yes, sir!" we shouted.

"Why don't you whisper in my ear? I can't hear you!"

We raised our voices several decibels. "Sir, yes, sir!"

"That's better." The sergeant approached one of the recruits to my right. "What's your name, private?"

"Renko."

"Just plain ol' Renko, huh? What happened to the 'sir' I just told you? Say it, boy."

"Sir, yes, sir!"

"You're going to give me some trouble, aren't you, boy?"

"Sir, no, sir."

"Would you like to demonstrate some push-ups to us right now?"

"No, sir, sir."

"But of course you do. Get down."

While Renko was counting out his push-ups, the sergeant approached me. "Where you from, private?"

"San Gabriel Valley, sir," I yelled.

"*Sir*, San Gabriel Valley, sir!"

"*Sir*, San Gabriel Valley, sir!"

"That make you some kind of tough boy?"

"No, sir."

"*Sir*, no, sir."

"*Sir*, no, sir!"

"Would you like to do some push-ups too?"

"Sir, no, sir!"

"Then you answer 'sir' every time I talk to you! You understand me?"

"Sir, yes, sir!"

"Keep it up, private. You're going to do outstanding."

The sergeant wasn't so positive later in the day when he screamed in my face, his spit stinging my eyes. "You little _____! I'm gonna make a man out of you if it takes the rest of my life. And from the looks of *you*, it'll take twice that long!" I could feel the rage boiling inside me, but I wisely controlled my temper.

The daily grind helped release some of my anger: Marching, working, sweating, climbing, shooting, crawling. We were on the go nonstop for 17 hours every day, with dust in our mouths and curses filling our ears. If we were supposed to be the "few good men" the Marine Corps was always seeking, it was no wonder there weren't very many.

Much as I wanted to flail at the sergeants who always yelled and swore at us, I knew better than to attack men who carried a higher rank than I. Besides, there was another motivation driving me: I always had to finish first. My pride in physical strength, so carefully fostered in high school, was now channeled to win in every drill—to run the fastest, to finish the obstacle course first, to do the most chin-ups, to shoot the most bull's-eyes. By graduation I had achieved the highest ranking in my class and had won a promotion to private first class.

Twelve weeks of basic training were followed by infantry instruction. With the Vietnam War in full swing, every Marine had to be prepared for the worst, so we "grunts" were given extensive training in jungle warfare. But now there were occasional leaves, and I used the time to good advantage with Sharon. I could tell she was crazy about me, and I couldn't stand to be away from her. Sharon had started college, so when I was home I drove her to school in the morning and waited outside her building as she attended class. At least this kept me out of trouble.

Finally training was finished, and our orders arrived in late November. Most of my buddies were being sent to safe, interesting places: Europe, other posts in the United States, even Hawaii. But my news was different. I could hardly believe my eyes as I read "Westpac." We all knew what that dreaded word meant.

Raul Ries was on his way to Vietnam.

6

A License To Kill

San Diego. It seemed like I always passed through this Southern California port city when something significant happened in my life. Tijuana was just a stone's throw away. There I had first met my American relatives and had joyously left with them, passing through San Diego on the way to our new home in Los Angeles. In Tijuana, despite my angry protests, my parents had ended their lengthy separation. In Tijuana I had boarded the ill-fated bus that was supposed to take me forever to Mamacita's home.

Now, on December 7, 1966, I was passing through San Diego again. I'd already said my goodbyes to Sharon, preferring not to endure a tearful farewell on the dock. Dad, Xavier, and Tom had driven me back to Camp Pendleton to meet the bus. At this moment, with his son leaving for war, Dad was quiet and contemplative. Faced with the fact that I might be killed, our feuds now seemed insignificant.

Alone I strode up the gangway of the U.S.S. *Gaffey*, ignoring the young Marines making tearful farewells

with their families. I stowed my seabags in their designated place and heard the idling engines shift into gear.
As the ship began to move, I returned to the deck to
watch as the dock shrank away behind us. Soon we
were moving steadily westward into the Pacific. "Do
you think we'll ever see America again?" a sad-eyed
private next to me asked anyone who might be
listening.

"I dunno, man." I abruptly turned and walked away,
not wanting to talk to anyone. The strange new fear
of never coming home again gripped us all. It wasn't
a question of philosophy or theology, of going to heaven
or going to hell. It was simply a question: *Will I live
through Vietnam?*

But there was another perspective. As the mainland
faded from view, most of the men were dwelling on
the potential of death. I concentrated on the thought
of returning home—as a hero.

Our journey lasted two weeks. We stopped for 48
hours in Okinawa. There all the tension we had felt
on board the ship exploded. Our brief leave sent us into
a frenzy of drinking, fighting, and carousing. Then we
returned to the monotony of the sea.

Five days out of Okinawa we caught our first sight
of Vietnam. We docked in Da Nang, and immediately
I noticed a unique smell—a hot, musty mixture of jet
fuel and explosives. As we received our orders, a chill
raced down my spine. My destination was the First
Marine Division, Alpha Company—better known as the
bounty hunters. Their job was to flush out the enemy
from jungle hideouts. It was one of the most dangerous assignments possible.

From Da Nang we were airlifted to Chu Lai. There
trucks transported us to the front lines. We almost
didn't make it. I felt our truck swerve and looked down

to see that we had barely missed a booby trap. The truck behind us wasn't so lucky.

We arrived at the front on December 24, just in time for the Christmas cease-fire. That damp, disgusting smell was even more intense. Occasionally gunfire could be heard. One question taunted us all: *What will it be like?* We acted out children's war games in our minds, but we recognized that this wasn't a game.

Christmas eve was quiet in our hooches. We kept to ourselves, each Marine lost in Christmases past. My memories started with glittering trees, beautiful presents, and laughter, then gradually darkened as I remembered my father's drinking and the never-ending fights. Were my parents fighting again right now? Well, so what if they were? I was a million miles away. *No big loss,* I bitterly decided. Along with several other soldiers, I got drunk.

Suddenly the old anger had returned to the surface, and in it I found new courage. At home I'd had to control my rage. I couldn't strike out at just anyone, and there was always the chance of being caught by the law. Now I had a license to kill. It was going to be either "Charlie" or me. I'd never yet lost a fight, and I wasn't going to lose this one either.

The day after Christmas, life returned to "normal." I was designated "point man." That meant I would walk 50 to a hundred yards ahead of our platoon to draw enemy fire and spot booby traps. We were assigned to set up an ambush that night outside a nearby village. We surrounded the little group of huts, hiding in the bushes. As darkness deepened, we watched the trails, keeping an eye out for Viet Cong coming or going.

The hours passed with agonizing slowness. My eyes,

unaccustomed to such intense concentration, began to see movement. "What was that?"

"Nothing. I don't see anything," answered an experienced partner. I squirmed at the thought that I might be hallucinating. By daybreak it seemed like everything was in motion—yet no one had appeared all night. *No action,* I thought. *Maybe this isn't going to be so bad after all.*

My sense of relief was short-lived. Marine intelligence had learned of Viet Cong hiding in another village. We were ordered to flush them out. We approached the village through the surrounding rice paddies. All at once the sound of bullets rang through the muggy air. "Get down!" someone barked.

Bullets pinged off the dikes, zinging off the water. I would pull myself up, shoot in the direction of the village, then flatten my body in the mud as the firefight blazed all around us. "Send in the big boys!" someone yelled over the radio. "We're under attack." Soon artillery and Phantom Jets were unloading their deadly cargo.

For six hours we had to lie in the mud, and the leeches took full advantage of our position, latching onto any available patch of skin. "You've got to ignore them," an experienced Marine told me. "They'll drive you crazy if you don't. Concentrate on the enemy." Finally we were able to rush the little village. But when we arrived and searched the huts, we found only a few women and children and some animals. The enemy had vanished into the surrounding jungle.

Such was the frustration of the war that we often couldn't see our enemy. Under such conditions I decided it wouldn't hurt to invoke the power of Deity, if it existed. Back at base camp I took a small picture of the Virgin Mary and set a candle in front of it. Here

I would hold a good-luck prayer ritual before going out to battle.

The next day we attacked another nameless village. All at once a Viet Cong ran out of one of the small hootches about 100 yards from me. I raised my M-16, aimed, and fired. His feet flew in the air and he landed headfirst in the dust.

With a tingle of anticipation I rushed to the fallen enemy and turned him over. A bloody mess was all that remained of his face. A vague fear disappeared in the pleasure of my first kill. There was no sadness in the fact that I had taken a life. It was him or me, and I had won.

From that moment on, hunting Viet Cong became a pleasure. My inner rage had found its perfect expression. Killing was the ultimate "win," and I began to enjoy it immensely. As I performed my daily prayer ritual in front of the Virgin, I also thought, "How many kills can I get today?" Death carried no fear for me. If I died, I died. No big deal.

The irony of this was that the military leadership "understood" that Americans were not loading their weapons unless fired upon. However, we rank-and-file soldiers understood that if you wanted to survive and return home, you always kept your weapons loaded and aimed. Any Vietnamese male over 13 years of age was fair game. Shooting him could possibly save an American life.

Our days became identical copies: another sweep, another ambush, another sniper. At night most of the guys were stoned out of their minds. Drugs were readily available, but for some reason they never appealed to me. Maybe killing was enough of a high.

Ron didn't care for the drugs either, so we often would talk during those lulls in the fighting. Our conversations drifted from harsh recounts of daily violence to gentle talk about friends and family we had left behind. Sometimes we would think about buddies who had been killed, such as a private we'd nicknamed "Scrooge" who had stepped on a mine. We never found any of his remains. "It could happen to us," Ron said soberly one night. I agreed, but said, "We can't worry about it. If it happens, it happens."

Often Ron and I would sit silently together and read letters from home. Sharon wrote to me a couple of times a week, and I answered by telling her how beautiful she was and that when I finished my tour of duty I was going to come home and marry her.

In response to my mention of marriage, Sharon wrote that while she liked me very much and enjoyed our friendship, she couldn't marry me. "I want to marry a Christian," she said.

I immediately answered, "I *am* a Christian. What did you think I was?" She tried to explain that a Christian is a person who has committed his life to Jesus Christ. I responded by saying that I'd always gone to church. "When we get married," I wrote, "we'll go to your church every Sunday." And then I reminded her of how much I missed her and couldn't wait to see her again.

Ron and I often listened to the radio broadcasts that floated in from Saigon. Sometimes I'd hear the popular song "Windy" and Sharon's beautiful face would fill my mind. Tears would sting my eyes and I knew, for the first time in my life, that I was in love. Would I ever see her again? She was reason enough to stay alive.

Soon all the Marines were mobilized in a massive campaign called Operation Arizona. We were to do a massive sweep of all the villages to the north, clearing them of Viet Cong. One morning Ron was walking the point and I was immediately behind him. He had only two months left before he was scheduled to return home, and I had protested his appointment to the point. Why should he take such a risk when he was so close to the end?

As we approached a village, Ron left the road and entered the bushes to conceal our ambush. He never saw the booby trap. As an explosion ripped through the jungle, I rushed to him. Twenty feet away I found one of his boots, his foot still in it. I pulled off my coat and placed it over the bloody stubs that were all that remained of his legs. "Are my legs gone?" he shouted in his delirium.

A couple of us found Ron's missing limbs and put them in a plastic bag for the medic. Then I grabbed Ron's rifle and senselessly charged the village. In a blind fury I shot at anything that moved. For me there was only one possible response to such an outrageous act: Anyone who had slanted eyes was going to pay for what happened to my friend.

The mutilation of Ron and other buddies fueled a growing hatred within me. There was no sense to this war. I hated the enemy, and even more I hated the government officials and military officers who lived so well, removed from the action, never having to look into the barrel of a gun or fear that with the next step they took they might be blown to bits. The loss of American life seemed absolutely senseless.

Personally, despite the many days I walked point, I managed to survive with minimal damage. There were always the leeches that gnawed at me, and occasionally the bites got infected and I had to be helicoptered to Da Nang Hospital for a day or two. One afternoon I was riding topside on an Amtrac-wheeler. I heard the familiar crack of sniper fire and felt a sharp blow in the back of my shoulder. A bullet had deflected off my flak jacket, leaving only a small burn on my skin as a reminder of its visit. Maybe Someone was looking out for me.

Whenever a fresh group of Marines was brought to our division, they would elect someone to serve as point man. After ten months at the front, I was ready to move toward the rear. When an 18-year-old Texan named Tony was selected to walk point in our platoon, I offered to break him in. The first morning I showed him how to slowly check the ground for deadly trip wires and false floors. Our ambush patrol outside a village was uneventful.

That night we were ordered to return and set up another ambush on the other side of the same village. This was a very dangerous operation, I explained. Once we'd been through a village, we could be sure the enemy had planted fresh booby traps. At night we had to check by stooping and feeling by hand. I went first, to show Tony, then suggested he do it. But he rushed the process and inadvertently tripped a wire. I saw a spark and yelled "booby trap!" I pushed him to try to avoid it, but too late. Both of us were thrown by the force of the explosion.

I was stunned for a moment. I checked my legs and arms, and they were all intact. Then I heard Tony moaning and got up to check him. His right arm and both of his legs were gone. By now the rest of the men had reached us, and we were suddenly engulfed in gunfire. The acrid smell of gunpowder stung my nostrils. I fell forward involuntarily, then pulled myself up. *Move ahead!* I commanded my body. I took a few more steps, then fell again.

"Ries! Get down, man. You're hit!" I couldn't tell who was yelling at me, but I was vaguely aware of pain in my back and leg. I stretched my hand around my midriff and brought it back. Blood. Too much blood! I could hear a chopper above, trying to pick up the injured, but enemy fire was keeping it away. Instinctively I stood up and fired in the direction of the enemy. Then, my head swimming as if I were in a twilight zone, I fell again.

The next thing I knew, I was in Da Nang Hospital. In surgery, the doctors took shrapnel from the grenade explosion out of my back and leg. But they were unable to remove all the pieces, and the next day I was transported to the hospital ship *Sanctuary* that was docked at Da Nang. That became my home for the next four weeks as the ship sailed to the Philippines.

No past fight or present fury could have prepared me for the carnage I saw on that dismal ship. Men lay row upon row, dismembered, disembowled, disfigured. As I walked through the wards, I saw men burned so badly by napalm that they no longer resembled human beings. There was a former football player named Jim; he had been shot in the head. His head was shaved bald, and he was hooked up to every conceivable life-support system. But he was a vegetable. One nurse told me he would probably never walk or even talk again.

I was stricken with horror at the sight of so many ruined lives. These were young kids—18, 19, 20 years old—but they would never live normal lives again. I was something of a novelty, since I didn't have my face burned off. My arms and legs were still in place. In no way was I maimed for life.

I was determined that Raul Ries would never again have the opportunity to be mutilated. I was going to go home alive, with my body intact. No more "walking point." No more war games.

During the last two weeks of my time aboard the

Sanctuary, we were docked in the Philippines. I was well enough then to go ashore for weekend liberty. Some nearly forgotten pastimes quickly regained their appeal, and motivated me even more to escape the war. As my recuperation drew to a close, I thought a lot about Sharon. Surely I would receive a medical discharge and be sent home. Sometimes I mentally sang the words of "Windy" and dreamed of the cool Southern California evenings. I thought of the laughs and good times with Tom and the Hessians. I could almost taste the hamburgers at the burger place. Even my folks became a more or less pleasant memory. "I'm going *home!*" I announced to the blank-faced paraplegic next to me. "No one can stop me. *No one.* Not even the President of the United States!"

Unfortunately, the U.S. Marine Corps wasn't as excited about my plans as I was. Though I still limped from the injuries, the doctor pronounced me fit for action and I was airlifted back to Vietnam. I was enraged. Why should I have to go back to the front? If the Marines were going to make me go back, then it was going to cost them. Someone was going to have to pay.

7

Taking The
Long Way Home

My passion for killing was gone. Despite my vehement objections to returning to the front, I was sent back to Alpha Company. The first couple of weeks I walked point again, and I tried to recapture the desire to kill. But now the dangers outweighed the excitement and adventure. I wanted to survive, and this was *not* the place to do it. I had to do something to get out of there.

Gradually I grew more willful and belligerent after 11 months of being in Vietnam. One night I grumbled to the sergeant, "If I keep going out there, I'll never make it home alive."

"So what are you going to do about it?" the sergeant grunted.

"I'm not going back out."

"You'll do what you're told."

"Why do I always have to walk the point?" I yelled. "Why doesn't someone else do it?"

"We're short of men, and you've got experience."

"You _____! I've had enough of this! I'm not going back out! You understand?"

"All right, all right...calm down."

"I'm not going to calm down, man. You go tell the captain to get me out of here."

A few minutes later I was told to report to the captain's hooch. I grabbed my M-16 and took it with me. "I understand you've got a problem," the captain said as I entered his tent.

"No, you've got the problem. I'm going to make this very clear." I spat out the words slowly and distinctly so he couldn't miss my message. "You send me out one more time...*one*...*more*...*time*...and somebody's gonna get hurt. And I don't mean Charlie. You got that?"

"You'll do what you're told, lance corporal."

"If you tell me to go out one more time, I'll kill you." I pointed my rifle at him to emphasize the point. "Do you understand."

"Yes, private." The captain took a piece of paper and wrote some orders. "Tomorrow I want you to go to Da Nang and see a psychiatrist."

"Great!" I answered. "Now you're thinking."

I repeated my threats to the military shrink. "If I don't get out now, man, there's gonna be trouble."

At first the doctor was sympathetic. But as I repeatedly defied him, he grew stern. "Look, Ries, you don't tell the U.S. Marine Corps what to do. You know that, don't you?"

"Let me tell you what I know!" I snapped back. "You send me back to the front and I *know* I'll kill you!" My voice was hard and cold. And I meant exactly what I said.

That psychologist handed me a slip of paper that was, in fact, my ticket out of Vietnam. But I wasn't home free—far from it. I was flown from Da Nang to Travis Air Force Base in Northern California. From there a military escort slapped handcuffs on me and drove me to Oakland Naval Hospital, where I was committed to the mental ward. For the next six months I was part of Project 49-A, the military label for Synanon, a popular group therapy program.

My group contained a mixture of problems. One man was struggling with homosexuality. Several others were hooked on drugs. An equal number were alcoholics. My problem was simple: I was boiling mad all the time. And nothing made me more angry than a bunch of people trying to "break" me.

The technique was simple: The group leader would choose a victim and attack. "What's your problem today?" he would demand. Usually the patient would respond, "I'm not going to tell you anything." Then it was open season for anyone in the group to attack the man verbally. They called him names, insulted him, harassed him. They forced their way into his private memories until he finally cracked. Then the patient would usually cry as he began to reveal the pain of his youth, abuse from parents, the mistakes he'd made. The idea was that once a person cracked, they could pick up the pieces and put him back together again. But I couldn't see how this process changed things. The victim of the abuse still had his problems. We never learned how to make a real, permanent change.

I thought the whole program was nonsense. I was not going to play the game. They tried every approach to make me crack. "You're a selfish loser, Ries," the leader said one morning. I responded with a slight smile.

"You're hiding the truth," said a former victim. "You're hiding it from us and you're hiding it from yourself."

I said nothing.

"You have an ego as big as the Pacific Ocean, Ries,"

chimed another patient. "You're disgusting."

"That's right, man," I laughed in his face. "What are you going to do about it?"

Shortly after I was committed to the hospital, I called my parents. The next morning they arrived for a visit—and with them was Sharon. I was still limping from my injuries, and this obviously touched her. "Raul, I've missed you so." She was almost whispering. Her hands warmly held mine, and her eyes never left my face.

Everyone wanted to know how I was doing. I didn't want them to know the real reason I was in the hospital, but I assured them it wasn't because of the injuries. "Everyone has to come here after Nam," I said.

"What are they doing to you?" Sharon asked.

"Oh, you know how they brainwash you when you go in. Well, now they have to make you normal again before they let you back into society." Everyone seemed to believe my story.

Because my parents were there, Sharon and I couldn't be alone, but before our brief visit was over I took her aside and told her how much I loved her. "I won't be here too long," I tried to assure her. "I'll keep in touch."

It was six more months before I saw her again. Day after day Dr. Williams and the group tried to break me, but I refused to crack. Their psychology was always asking us to look backward. I wasn't interested in anything my past had to offer. Why review all the painful arguments with my parents? Why think about all the senseless killing and my buddies getting blown to bits? All I wanted was a new start. I wanted to get out of the Marines, leave Vietnam behind, and begin a new life with Sharon.

I rebelled against every authority that tried to make me conform to the military rules. After breakfast each morning we were all supposed to clean our area of the hospital. I refused. "Ries, you son of a b_____, get out there and work," a male orderly would demand.

"No way, man!" I'd sneer.

"Who do you think you are?"

"I think I'm Raul Ries, man. *You* do the work."

Dr. Williams responded by informing me that my "liberty" had been "seized." Simply put, that meant no more trips to town. Before long I realized that cleaning up once a day was a fair trade for a few hours of freedom.

But nothing could make me play the group therapy game. Dr. Williams added private sessions to my agenda, but made no progress there either. What he didn't know, and what only Sharon saw a glimpse of through my letters, was that the suffering around me had an effect. Outwardly I remained belligerent, but inwardly I cried as I saw these men with broken hearts and broken spirits, trapped by their past and the horrors of war, many of them with no hope for a happy future. But I didn't see their condition as my own condition. I wanted no part of the Marines, and the only way I saw out was to refuse to play by their rules.

Finally Dr. Williams gave up. He called me in one day to tell me that he had written a letter to the Pentagon. "Do you want to know my conclusions?" he said.

"Yeah, why don't you tell me your conclusions?" I sneered.

"You're a phony. You staged this whole thing."

"Staged what?"

"The entire hate angle. You fabricated your insanity in order to get out of the service."

"I don't know what you're talking about."

"You know exactly what I'm talking about. You haven't fooled me. I've recommended a dishonorable discharge. You're to report to Camp Pendleton until the papers are processed." From his steely-eyed stare, I knew that he felt he had lost a bizarre battle with my will.

Camp Pendleton, where this two-year ordeal had all begun, was practically a jail. I immediately started breaking all the rules. I refused to press my uniform. I didn't show up for roll call. I didn't follow orders. Since I was getting a dishonorable discharge anyway, what difference did it make? Naturally, I had no weekend liberty.

I was removed from the main population, and while other marines marched and played war games, I was told to clean barracks and do other menial tasks. I did as little as possible, and someone was always watching me to keep me in line.

My confinement didn't keep me from leaving Camp Pendleton to see Sharon. One Friday night at sundown I approached the sergeant on duty at the barracks. "Hey, man, I'll give you 20 bucks if you let me out of here."

The sergeant sized me up coolly. "Let's see the money." I flashed a crisp bill which he quickly snapped from my hand. "Take off, sucker."

I quickly stepped out into temporary freedom and hitchhiked to Baldwin Park. My parents were amazed to see me. I offered no explanation but picked up the phone and dialed. Sharon answered.

"Raul! Where are you?"

"I'm coming to pick you up!"

"Wonderful! But how...?"

"We'll talk when I get there."

At last Sharon and I were together. So much loneliness and passion was locked inside us. But she exercised more control. "Please, Raul. I can't."

"Why not? I love you."

"I know you do. But please don't."

"Is it because of your religion?"

"Look, Raul—God created sex for marriage, and apart from marriage it will only bring heartache."

"I want to marry you."

"I can't get married yet. I'm still in college. My greatest desire is to go to Chile before I get married."

I backed off, but half-teasing I told her, "I'm going to get you pregnant. Then you'll have to marry me."

"What a joke!" she laughed. "You'll never get me pregnant."

A weekly pattern for our rendezvous was quickly established. Each Friday night, I would buy my way out of Camp Pendleton and head for Sharon's door. Monday morning I'd be back at camp in my angry state of insubordination. It was a strange charade, yet an anarchy for which I felt no guilt. All that mattered were those few hours with Sharon when all the cares of the world were swept away. My love for her was like a peaceful oasis in a wild sea of madness and mutiny. She quieted me. She soothed me. She seemed to understand, without explanation, what I had endured in Vietnam. I didn't tell her that my sleep was often punctuated by nightmares in which Charlie still stalked me. I would wake up in a cold sweat, reliving again and again the death of one buddy or another. I saw the mutilation of Ron. I heard the screams of men . . . the roar of artillery . . . the crackling pop of rifles. All of that faded when I was with Sharon.

On Easter weekend we planned to camp at the beach with some friends and family. Sharon picked me up in her mother's van and drove me to the beach. But no one else showed up. As the hour got later, Sharon grew increasingly nervous. I tried to comfort her with tender kisses. But she resisted my advances. "Why are you upset?" I quietly asked. "I'm not going to hurt you."

"I think we should go."

"Go where? Isn't this where everyone agreed to meet?"

"What will they think if they see us in the van together?"

"Why are you worried? Everyone knows we're in love."

Finally, sometime after midnight, Sharon could resist no longer and we enjoyed the most indescribable moment of passion. Never had I felt such joy, and it only motivated me more to have her forever.

Three weeks later, when I visited her home, she seemed much quieter. When her parents left the house for a few moments to run an errand, she started crying. "Hey, baby, what's the matter?" I asked.

"Raul...I..." her voice broke.

"What's wrong? Tell me..."

"I'm...I'm going to have a baby."

"Really! That's great!"

"I'm pregnant, Raul. You got me pregnant."

I picked her up and swung her around the room. What wonderful news! "Why are you crying, baby? We'll just get married." I set her down gently. "Will you marry me, Sharon?"

"Raul, you don't have to marry me. I'll understand. Don't feel you have to do it just because I'm pregnant."

"Are you crazy? I *want* to marry you."

Still crying, she whispered, "I just hope God can make it turn out all right."

I gently touched her chin and lifted it so her eyes met mine. "Of course it will be all right. We'll make it all right!" I asked her if her parents knew.

She shook her head to say no. "It would break their hearts."

"Well, don't worry. I'm sure I'll get leave for us to get married in a few weeks. Who knows? Maybe my discharge will come before that."

Within a few weeks wedding plans were quickly put together. Despite the way we became engaged, I was delighted. How I treasured Sharon! Somehow the emotional extremes of Vietnam had burned in me a deep and intense love for her. I was delighted to marry her. Now I could start life all over again. With Sharon at my side, I could be happy in my own house. We would have a peaceful home...like Mamacita's.

8

Broken Promises

Our wedding occurred on a clear and glorious July afternoon. Nearly 500 people packed the sanctuary for the festive occasion. Sharon kept the pregnancy a secret until after the wedding in order to spare her parents any embarrassment. I knew Sharon's father had wanted her to wait for marriage until she was finished with school. But when he saw she was determined to proceed with the wedding, he supported her totally. Her mother also acted as though nothing was wrong, yet there were little signs that indicated perhaps she knew Sharon's secret. Both of Sharon's parents reached out and welcomed me into their family. And my parents absolutely loved Sharon.

My discharge had not yet arrived at Camp Pendleton, but I managed to secure three days' leave for this special event. And as I stood tall and proud in front of the church, I watched the pretty bridesmaids, like delicate rays in a pastel rainbow, make their way to the altar. Then the music swelled and the congregation rose to its feet. Holding her father's arm, Sharon came toward me like a vision in white.

I was so thrilled to marry her! I knew she would be the perfect wife. As she moved gracefully down the aisle, I thought, *You're such a winner, Ries. You really scored this time!* As she reached the altar and took my hand, I could see that Sharon had been crying, but she was trying to cover it with a forced smile. We respectfully exchanged the vows that everyone says during weddings. I wasn't concentrating on the words, only on her beautiful face. "You're gorgeous," I whispered into her ear.

"Please, pay attention," she whispered back.

I'm sure at that moment I meant to love, honor, and cherish Sharon for the rest of my life. Sharon meant her vows too, but in a different way that I couldn't understand. It was as if she was saying them to someone else. Until the pastor presented us to the congregation as man and wife, it was as if she didn't even know I was there. Then suddenly a radiant glow transformed her face, as if a light had been turned on inside her. She was weeping, but this time for joy. Never had I seen her so beautiful.

After waving farewell to everyone and shaking the rice out of our clothes and hair, we happily disappeared to a quiet hotel. There we reveled in the privacy of being alone together. Everything seemed so perfect...until Monday morning, when I had to report back to Camp Pendleton.

Sharon found a cozy little apartment in Anaheim. There she hung colorful curtains, arranged the furniture, and prepared a nursery for our first child. I helped whenever I could buy my way out of Camp Pendleton. When she inquired about why I always arrived home so late, I told her that they didn't release us until after sundown. And then I would have to be back on the base before breakfast. Sharon never suspected that I was leaving the camp illegally, figuring my hours were normal for military men.

Fortunately, this situation didn't last long. My discharge papers finally arrived from Washington in mid-August, and what a surprise! I could not believe it as I read the words: "Raul Ries is hereby declared honorably discharged from the United States Marine Corps by the convenience of the government." As I showed the notice to Sharon, I couldn't help but think that this was a miracle. There was no other explanation. I had enlisted for four years and had served only two. When Dr. Williams had told me his conclusions, there was no reason to expect an honorable discharge, especially considering my behavior at Camp Pendleton.

At last I was free to begin life again. It wasn't hard for me to make a living. I was a hustler and quickly landed two jobs in Los Angeles as a courier for two banks. As always, I was friendly and forever smiling. Everyone liked Raul Ries.

But I had no intention of doing such menial work for long. In the evenings Sharon and I would share our private dreams. I wanted to go to college and also return to the martial arts. With a couple of years of dedication to kung fu, I believed I could achieve a black belt. Then I would open my own kung fu studio and we'd be rolling in the dough. However, I wanted to continue developing until I achieved an eighth-degree black belt, which signified a master of the martial arts—the highest level possible.

Sharon supported me in my dream, seeing it as a healthy way to channel the desire to fight that I'd had for so many years. Her dream was to return to Latin America, where she had lived for so many years.

"Great!" I told her. "We can move to Mexico or Chile and I'll open a kung fu studio there."

Knowing that religion was such an important part of her life, I encouraged Sharon to find a church for us to attend on Sundays. And most Sundays both of us attended. It wasn't the highlight of my week, but I didn't mind it too much.

In those first months of marriage my anger seemed dormant. Occasionally I still overreacted to rude drivers on the freeway. And I still had thoughts of physical violence when people got pushy with me. But mostly I was content just to be a hard-working young breadwinner, and I threw myself wholeheartedly into the process.

Our wedding and the prospect of a grandchild more or less mended my relationship with my parents. My folks were very visible at our wedding, and periodically they would drop by to spend a few hours with us in Anaheim. Our relationship was calm, although very superficial—until the day my dad showed up at the apartment with a six-pack of beer under his arm.

When I saw that six-pack, memories of my childhood flooded my mind. If I let my father in the house and he started to drink, I knew that within a couple of hours his personality would change. He would start cursing, sticking verbal barbs in us, abusing my mother...I wanted nothing to do with that man. I put up my hand before he could enter: "Hey, man! You can't drink beer in my house."

My father couldn't believe what he'd just heard. "What did you say?"

"You heard me. You can't bring that beer into my house."

"Well, look at that! My own son won't let me into his home. What's the matter? You think you're too good for me? Let me tell you something. I can drink anywhere I want . . .''

As Dad began to verbally assault me, I felt the old rage begin to rumble within. Slowly it grew, that familiar desire to solve this problem with my fists. "Get out of my house," I said, trying not to betray my full anger. Out of the corner of my eye I could see Sharon withdraw from the room, fear draining the color from her face. Her fear made me more enraged. "You won't drink in *my* house. This is *my* home. *I* pay the rent. You take your _____ booze and get out!"

"Oh, I get it! That little woman you've married has you tied to her apron. She's so religious and you're not man enough to stand up to her."

"You keep Sharon out of this!" My fist was clenched, eager for action. "If you ever say or do anything to hurt her, I'll kill you." I spoke the words coldly, with absolute clarity. I couldn't have been more serious.

For a moment we stared at each other. Then Dad backed up. As he and Mom headed to their car he systematically hurled every curse and insult he'd ever used on me, plus a few new ones I'd never heard him use before.

After that incident, the only contact with my parents was a few uncomfortable times when Sharon pushed me to make a visit. I would rather have avoided them altogether, for I had Sharon and felt no need for any other family. Sharon, having come from a close and loving home, couldn't understand why I wanted to avoid my parents, even when our visits ended with angry words.

It might have helped if we could have talked about my feelings. But this was a part of me that couldn't open up, so Sharon never heard me talk about my anger and fears. In addition to my family, I was haunted by the memories of Vietnam. Occasionally I would have a nightmare and be back in the rice paddies with those bloodsucking leeches latching themselves to my body and my ears ringing from a bombing raid. And then I'd see Ron or Tony or some other buddy blown to bits and I'd have to pick up dismembered limbs and pieces of their bodies and put them into plastic bags. . . and I'd wake up to the sound of my screaming voice. Sharon would hold me and tell me, "You're okay, Raul. Nothing is going to hurt you."

Late one December night Sharon called me at work. "Raul. . . meet me at the hospital. I think the baby's coming!" With the anxious optimism that all first-time parents experience, I drove quickly to the hospital. I was nervous. . . excited. . . unable to sit still. A few hours later Raul Ries, Jr., came into the world, crying lustily.

The birth of a child is forever a miracle to me. The first time I held my little boy, there was a new spot of tenderness in my heart. I examined his tiny face and marveled at the perfection of his little hands and feet. I felt grateful, thankful, and glad to be alive.

The hurts of the past were temporarily abandoned. My parents and Sharon's family all descended on our small hospital room. Sharon's nightstand and dresser were banked with cascades of blue and white flowers. Sunlight filtered through the spotless windows, celebrating our joy with us.

I went home that night and crawled into bed. Sleep came quickly after the exhausting day. And in my peaceful dreams I saw the tired yet exhilarating smile of my wife as she held our son. Already she'd forgotten the hours of pain from pushing little Raul into the world. Then our eyes had locked and we had felt a oneness. Slowly that wholesome image of Sharon faded and was replaced by the hideous picture of a Vietnamese mother, a silent scream frozen on her face as she clutched her newborn infant. Both were lying dead in the mud.

I escaped from the nightmare and found myself in the dark apartment, drenched in sweat. A sick feeling in my gut kept me awake the rest of the night. Guilt began to gnaw at me. I tried to shove it aside. "I was just doing my job...that's all." I spoke at the invisible memory with defensive harshness. But my conscience was not convinced. My son's birth had provided a tragic new perspective of my violent past.

The first few sleepless, blissful weeks with little Raul helped me break the pattern of attending church. With two jobs, junior college, and kung fu classes, it became easy to sleep in on Sunday mornings, my only day off. Sometimes Sharon would slip out to early service and return before I was up so we could enjoy the day together.

Six months after the birth of Raul, Sharon learned that she was pregnant again. One evening she wondered aloud, "Why don't we move back to the Covina area?" It wasn't a plea, just a gently expressed wish. I watched her as she sat rocking Raul to sleep. A soft smile graced her mouth. I knew that being close to her mother would make this special time even more precious to her.

Since I was working in Los Angeles, it didn't really matter where we lived. In fact, my commuting time could be cut in half if we lived in the San Gabriel Valley. I thought about the move with growing interest. "You're right, babe. Let's check it out."

Within weeks we were resettled in Covina, and I decided to take a new job at the grocery store where I'd worked as a kid. Our little family fit nicely into the young, residential community where we rented an apartment: There were other babies and other newly-wed couples. And just a phone call away were my old friends. It was fun having a baby, and nice looking forward to another. Yet there was a growing restlessness. I missed the excitement of those days when I was the toughest kid in Baldwin Park, West Covina, and the surrounding area. There was no ego gratification in stocking store shelves and working the cash register all day and then trying to quiet a crying kid at night.

One evening while Sharon was shopping, I dialed a familiar number. "Tom? Hey, it's Raul! How you doing?"

"Raul! Where are you? It's great to hear your voice!"

"I'm at home. Sharon and I just moved back to Covina." I wasn't particularly anxious to fill Tom in on the details of my middle-class, family-man life. So I quickly asked, "What have you been up to?"

"I just got back from Nam. Got shot in the rear."

"What?"

"I'm not kidding, man. I got a AK-47 in the rear. It really messed up my leg. At least it doesn't keep me from riding a motorcycle. Hey, what are you doing Friday night?" The bitterness in Tom's voice diminished as he told me that some of the old gang were going over to the burger place. "Why don't you cruise by?"

"Hey, great! See you then, man."

Soon Sharon returned home, laden with disposable diapers and groceries. I started to tell her about Tom, then caught myself. *What she doesn't know won't hurt her*, I concluded.

The rest of the week I looked forward to seeing the guys again. Friday night I told Sharon that I had to run some errands and I'd be back in a few hours. She looked puzzled as she kissed me goodbye.

At the burger place, it felt as if nothing had changed. Six of us devoured hamburgers and cracked up reliving the "good old days." We reminisced about the fights, the chicks, and the scrapes with the cops. And by the time the night was over, we'd relived a few of those adventures.

I arrived home at 2:00 A.M. My shirt was ripped from a minor fight. I'd been drinking a little. Sharon was waiting up, her eyes red from crying. "Where have you been?" she asked, her voice sad and scared.

"I've been out." With that curt explanation I brushed past her and went to bed.

The next morning Sharon tried to talk to me again. "Where were you? Why were you out half the night? Why didn't you call me?" She was hurt, but there was a reserved anger in her tone. I hadn't told Sharon about my sordid past and I wasn't about to start now. I knew she wouldn't approve of my nocturnal activities. So the more she tried to force an explanation, the more defensive I became. Finally, in frustration, I shoved her out of my way and headed for the front door. Seven months pregnant, she barely kept her balance as she caught herself against a chair.

I returned to a stony silence in our apartment that night. And for a moment I felt guilty. "Hey, I'm sorry. I didn't mean to push you. You okay?" She nodded to tell me she was. "I ran into some old friends last night," I explained. "It's no big deal."

But the old lifestyle of Raul Ries had been reignited, and I began to see Tom and my old buddies regularly. When Sharon protested my late hours, I would think, *She doesn't want me to have any fun.* Her complaints fueled an already smoldering fire. The old rage was back, and nothing was going to keep me from expressing it on some unfortunate soul.

Sometimes it was Sharon. Our honeymoon existence rapidly deteriorated into a hotbed of arguments and confrontations. More and more frequently I would pinch Sharon's arm or neck, or yank her across the room, or shove her against a wall. In spite of these actions, I felt pretty good about the fact that I never really belted her. I mean, my mom got it a lot worse from my dad. Still, when she'd cry, I would say I was sorry, but after awhile Sharon began to say, "Why do you say you're sorry when you're going to do it again? Don't say you're sorry. Change, and then I'll *know* you're sorry."

Within a year after little Shane was born, we were no longer a happy family. I was growing more and more distant. And to compensate, Sharon began spending more time at church. Occasionally she would ask me to go with her because it was hard packing two little boys to church alone. But I'd remind her that with my busy schedule—I was now working long hours, attending school, and carrying a heavy load of kung fu lessons and practices—this was my only chance to sleep late. Sharon added a midweek Bible study to her church activity, and many nights I'd come home and find her curled up in her favorite chair, reading her Bible and praying. This made me furious, even though she always put her Bible down when I entered the front door, and sometimes I'd cut her down with acid comments that accused her of thinking she was better than I just because she was more religious.

In the midst of our domestic turmoils, there was a strong guilt growing inside me. I was well aware that Sharon was a fabulous wife and mother. Our children were loved, well-dressed, and secure, in spite of my inconsistent involvement with them. Our house was always immaculate. Sharon even made sure to serve me her special vegetable soup, and my favorite meal—steak with hot sauce. The more I saw her loving me, the more I realized that I didn't deserve her love. I was a liar and a cheat. I was abusive and unfaithful to my wife. My nightmares regularly reminded me that I was also a murderer. It was obvious to me that I was no good and I could never change. And yet my wife loved me. I could see something inside her—a joy, a peace—that made no sense when I thought about her circumstances.

While I felt inadequate, and knew I was a lousy husband, I didn't feel bad enough to change my ways. In fact I really didn't think I could change. I came and went whenever I felt like it. If I wanted to stay out late and Sharon needed an explanation, I told her I had to work late at the store to stock shelves, or that I had a kung fu practice.

One night the phone rang as we were finishing dinner. Sharon answered it and heard a feminine voice plaintively ask, "Is Raul there? I need to talk to him."

"Who's calling?" Sharon asked quietly.

"This is Shelley. Who are you? His sister?"

"I'm his wife."

"His *wife*? You've got to be kidding!" The girl broke into gales of laughter before she hung up.

"Raul, who's Shelley?" Sharon asked coldly as she too-carefully replaced the telephone receiver. I said nothing, trying to figure how quickly I could escape from her wrath. *"Who is Shelley?"* Desperation filled her voice and tears began to course down her face.

"That _____. She's nobody. Nobody." I was at a loss for words.

"You're sleeping around, aren't you?" Sharon shouted.

"Hey, calm down," I said, getting up from the table

to hold her. "You know you're my only girl."

Sharon pulled away from my advance. "Then who was that who called?"

"Probably some chick who ran into me at the store. I guess she got my number. It's no big deal. Don't worry."

"You must have led her on."

"No, no. I don't know where she got the idea to call me." I had lied so many times that I was a master, and Sharon finally calmed down and believed my explanation. Another crisis was avoided.

The conflicts at home further motivated me to intensify my efforts in kung fu. Under the instruction of Jimmy Woo, I quickly progressed. I was naturally quick, and violent—two attributes that served me well in the martial arts. Sharon protested the money I spent for lessons on our limited income, but I tried to explain that it was an investment in our future. Then in January of 1971 I earned my black belt. That prompted me to cut back my hours of work at the supermarket so I could prepare to open my own studio.

Sharon was pleased with my achievement until I told her, "You're going to have to get a job! The store cut back my hours." That was a lie, but I couldn't risk her refusing. "Now that I have my black belt, it's a good time to start my own kung fu studio. But I can't make it happen if you're sitting around all day doing nothing. You'll need to earn some bucks until we get on our feet."

The news was not well-received. "Raul...what about the kids?"

"What about them?" I snapped. I couldn't understand how Sharon wrapped herself up in our children. Outside of her church activities, the kids were her world. "I just need you to work for a couple of years. Help me rent a place, and when we start making big bucks, you can quit.''

''But how can I leave the kids? They're so little.''

''Come on—they're two and three years old. You're just too lazy to work.''

Sobs surged from deep inside my wife. ''How can you do this to me?'' she whispered hoarsely. ''How can you make me leave my babies?''

I could not understand her emotional outburst. However, I was nervous, afraid she might refuse my demands. So I softened my tone of voice. ''Honey, I'm not asking you to put the boys up for adoption. Just help me out a little. You won't have to work for long. I promise.''

So Sharon went to work as a secretary. Every morning she got up, dressed and fed Raul Junior and Shane, dropped them off at the next-door neighbor's house, and clocked in at her job. She came home for lunch to save money. One noon hour I found her sobbing, her head cradled in her arms. ''What's your problem?'' I asked coldly.

''Marge doesn't want me to see my boys when I come home for lunch. She says it's their nap time and if I come by they'll be all excited and she won't be able to calm them down after I leave.'' I stared at Sharon and saw her pitiful expression, her eyes wet and swollen. But I felt no pity. I was angry that she couldn't act any stronger. ''Raul . . .'' she looked up at me. ''Don't you have a heart inside you? Don't you care about anyone but yourself? Don't you care about *anyone*?''

I shuffled around momentarily. ''Listen,'' I finally said, ''I've got a kung fu class to teach in ten minutes. You get some rest. Okay? You'll feel better.''

For a moment our eyes met and we held each other's gaze. For the first time I noticed that the joy she had always reflected was gone and in its place was a hard-ened bitterness. For an instant I thought that I should be concerned, but I quickly rejected that thought. With-out a word I turned and rushed out the door. As the screen door slammed behind me, I muttered, "Women. What do they want, anyway? You can't make them happy."

9

A Second Shot At Life

A handful of seasons came and went. Spring returned, bringing a pelting rain against the bedroom windows. It was a Saturday afternoon, and I was sitting cross-legged on our king-size bed, surrounded by books and magazines about the martial arts. I had mastered many of the physical aspects of kung fu from Jimmy Woo, but I had heard from other instructors that one could gain incredible power by adding Eastern mysticism from Zen Buddhism. However, despite my efforts, I had trouble doing even the most basic form of Eastern meditation.

With the house quiet, I closed my eyes and focused on my breathing. Then I tried to empty my mind. "Breathe deeply," I reminded myself. "Breathe deeply with a circular motion.... Now exhale." I began to feel a slight sense of detachment. Inhale. Exhale.

"Give me that, Shane!" Little Raul's angry words cut through the silence. *Those _____ kids!* I muttered to myself. I slammed the books shut in frustration. How could I ever develop the kind of inner powers my martial arts philosophy offered? I couldn't get past stage one. "It's the stupid kids," I griped to myself. "Every time I begin to gain that sense of detachment, they open their big mouths."

Deep inside, though, I knew this wasn't the problem. Something else was preventing me from tapping my psychic "force." *Sharon's probably praying that I won't be able to do it,* I thought. *She's probably afraid I'll kill her if I get any more power.*

No doubt she was praying. We had moved to a pretty house in a nice, clean neighborhood. Sharon had to work for over two years before quitting her job. My dream of a kung fu studio had come true, and already I was developing larger and larger classes. My brother Xavier had even participated in the venture with me—until Dad made him believe that I was trying to rip him off of his share of the business. But the split with Xavier hadn't hurt the studio. Every week I enrolled new students and happily collected their money.

Our family life was another story. My parents and I had declared all-out war. And a freezing chill had settled between Sharon and me. She was deeply involved in her church now, and her faith seemed to have strengthened her, calming her outbursts. Instead of confronting me, she kept her distance, probably out of sheer terror. She and the kids lived in one world and I in another. Ironically, I still loved Sharon. Despite my unfaithfulness, I had never loved any other woman, and I couldn't even comprehend the thought of losing her.

When our paths crossed, Sharon and I were usually civil. But when there was a disagreement, whatever little self-control I'd once had was completely gone. The anger came instantly, in a furious rush. Time and again

I shoved, pushed, and even slugged Sharon. Afterward I felt no remorse for my actions, believing that she had only received what she deserved.

One evening we were looking at some old photographs. In her album was a page of old boyfriends. "They were all just friends," Sharon assured me. "You're the only one I had a crush on." But I became enraged with jealousy and ripped the page out of her book and tore it up.

"Oh, so that's the game," Sharon said, annoyed by my action. She opened one of my albums and shredded a page of my old girlfriends.

Fury instantly possessed me. I picked up our heavy wedding album and hurled it into her face. Her glasses shattered. She began to scream uncontrollably as blood trickled down her cheeks. "That's what you get for always bugging me!" I shouted as I stormed into my office and slammed the door.

Fortunately, the glass only cut Sharon's nose. Later she gently tried to explain how she could have been seriously hurt, even blinded. "Aw, c'mon," I said, "I'd never blind you." I had seen my mom take worse shots than that, and she had survived.

A few weeks later as Sharon was preparing to leave for church, I politely asked her to stay. "Let's do something together," I said.

"You're welcome to come with us," she said as she finished putting a jacket on Shane.

"I've got to be at the studio in an hour."

"I need to get out," she said, holding Shane in her arms. "This is my only chance to get to church this week."

"You and your _____ church!" I shouted as I gave her a sharp kung fu kick just above her knee. She buckled from the blow and just barely managed to break her fall so as not to hurt Shane. I stormed out of the room, letting her limp to the car with the two boys.

Later that day she again tried to explain how I'd hurt her. "Your kicks are so powerful now. You could have broken my leg," she pleaded.

"Nah, I wouldn't do that."

"Raul, I can't take this much longer. You're hurting me. The kids live in constant fear of you. All we get from you are curses and yelling and abuse. You never think about anyone except yourself."

"Hey! I make a good living, don't I? I got you a nice house. You don't have to work anymore."

"If you don't stop this abuse, I'm going to have to take the boys and leave you."

Fear gripped me with those words. The one thought I could not bear was the idea of losing Sharon and the boys. This was not the first time she had mentioned leaving, and each time my reaction was the same. The thought of another man taking her and loving her, and my boys calling someone else "Daddy"...that I would *never* allow. We would die first.

I grabbed Sharon's arm and squeezed it hard. "You're hurting me!" she said as she tried to pull away. With her free hand she took off her glasses and tossed them onto the couch.

"You listen to me," I hissed, squeezing her arm even harder. "If you leave, I'll kill you. And I'll kill *him*. And I'll kill the boys. So don't get any big ideas. You'll never live to see them come true!" I meant what I said, and Sharon knew it.

Sharon wasn't the only one forced to deal with my growing violence. Even my kung fu activities couldn't satiate my drive. I would stare people down at stop signs, hoping to stir up some action. Sometimes I would walk up to strangers and try to establish eye contact. If anyone got defensive, I attacked.

One night Sharon and I headed over to my mom's. A block from the house I drove into a little neighborhood market. "I'm thirsty for a Coke," I told her. "You want anything?" She shook her head, so I jumped out of the car and headed for the door. About that time a man strolled across the parking lot and passed Sharon's side of the car. He glanced at her and moved on toward the door. Jealousy surged inside me. "What are you looking at, sucker?" I shouted. "That's my wife you're checking out!"

He looked puzzled and annoyed. "I wasn't looking at—"

Without giving him a chance to continue, I grabbed him by the shirt and shoved him against the wall.

"Raul!" Sharon shrieked. "Come on! Let's go!"

I pounded the man's head against the wall two or three times. "I'm taking my wife home, sucker. Then I'll be back to deal with you!"

After one last slam, I leaped into the car and peeled out. Sharon was stunned: "He didn't even look at me."

"Shut up and get out!" I ordered, screeching to a stop in front of my parents' house. Then I burned rubber all the way back to the market while I visualized myself tearing the intruder to pieces. But when I got back to the market he was gone. "Chicken _____," I muttered as I left, disappointed.

Except for occasional episodes like that, Sharon suffered alone. Her bruises were never obvious, and she never told anyone about her problems. Her parents, I'm sure, sensed what was happening, but they never said anything about it, which only made me angrier. "Every time your folks come over here, it's the same old thing," I'd tell Sharon. "All they do is hug me and tell me how much they love me. And they're always smiling. It makes me sick. What's your dad think he is, Santa Claus?''

When Sharon's parents visited her and the grandchildren, I usually tried to make sure I was not home. On Saturday evening, the day before Easter, I missed my chance to slip out the back door before they arrived. "Raul, why don't you come with us tomorrow night?" her mother said after giving me a hug. "We're going down to Calvary Chapel in Costa Mesa."

"What's that? Some kind of church?" I sneered.

She ignored my tone of voice. "Well, yes, it's a church. But it's not like any other church you've ever seen."

"How so?"

"Well, this guy Chuck Smith is the pastor. And he has a real special love for young people. He really speaks their language."

"What language is that?" I smiled cynically at my little joke. My mother-in-law chuckled, without taking the slightest offense. "Hey, I hate to rush out, but I've got to meet a couple of students I'm tutoring over at the studio." No one flinched at my obvious lie. Then, as I walked out the door, I added, "Sorry I can't make it tomorrow night. Maybe some other time." I spent the next few hours with Tom and the guys, until I was sure my Christian in-laws were gone and Sharon and the kids were probably in bed.

The next morning I arose early, facing a full Sunday schedule of kung fu demonstrations and lessons. Sharon and the kids were trying to get ready for church while I was rushing around myself. Raul made the mistake of getting in my way as I scurried down the hall dripping wet, covered only by a towel. "Why don't you watch where you're going?" I snapped at him.

"You watch where *you're* going!" Raul snapped back,

glaring belligerently at me. His five-year-old body was rigid with defiance.

"You little _____!" I grabbed him roughly by the waist and hurled him toward the end of the hall. He landed in a screaming heap.

Sharon charged out of the bedroom, terror etched on her face. She ran to Raul's side, picked him up, and rocked him in her arms. Her tears mingled with his as she tried to explain why his father had attacked him with such violence.

Sharon didn't say a word to me, but cast one long, intent look my direction as she carried her sobbing son to his room. When she finally reemerged, she sized me up again, silently. There was a new determination in her face—a kind of calm finality I had never seen before. It should have frightened me, but my mind was already redirected toward arriving at the studio by 10:30, in time to prepare for my first class.

As I drove away, I felt vaguely sorry that I'd lost my temper with Raul. He really was a good little guy. *Maybe next time he'll stay out of my way.* I smiled a little, figuring I'd taught him a lesson. Even so, I wished the ugly incident had never happened.

My kung fu classes went smoothly that day. And to top it off, a pretty new blue-eyed student made sure I knew her name and phone number before she left. I drove home that night feeling good about life.

And so it was that I arrived at my home to be greeted by a locked door, a messy backyard, my weights in the trash, and, once I broke into the house . . . packed suitcases. Sharon was finished with me. I knew she meant business. There was no time to think. My mind was already programmed by the jealousy, rage, and guilt that had injected their powerful poisons in me for so many years. There was no use fighting them any longer.

Peace would never be possible. The .22 rifle promised the only solution to my profound despair.

As I waited for Sharon and the boys to return, my hate turned into a desire to end our hate-marred existence!

My diabolical vigil began. The minutes ticked distinctly by on the clock that looked like a giant pocket watch sitting on top of our television. The quiet drove me mad. I flicked on the TV. A noisy commercial broke into the silence with an inane musical sales pitch. I quickly flipped the dial. A talk-show host was interviewing a vacant-eyed actress. I flipped again. Dan Rather—60 Minutes. I flipped again. A gentle, bald-headed man was talking. This seemed like the least obnoxious program on Sunday night TV.

Impatiently I sat down and stared at him, not the least bit interested in what he had to say. A few seconds later I jumped up again and peered out the window. Nothing was moving.

"This is the real sign of love. . ." The calm voice on TV cut through my grim preparations for death. ". . . in order to show love, God gave something that was special to Him, something of which there could be no replacement—His only begotten Son." I slowly moved back to the chair in front of the TV screen. "The purpose of that gift was that you might be able to fellowship with God, that you could experience His love, that you could come to know that love yourself, and to enjoy the benefits not just now, but forever. For He has offered to us eternal life through this gift of His Son, Jesus Christ." Despite the emotional message, the man never raised his voice.

"Jesus died on the cross for your sins. He took your guilt upon Himself. When they drove the nails into His hands and feet, He was taking *your* punishment. He was dying for all the wrong *you've* ever done in your life.'' As he described the crucifixion, I could see again the gruesome crucifix in front of the Catholic church I attended as a boy. *So that's what it was all about.*

But wait a minute. Who is this guy? How could he know about all the wrong things I've done? My guilty conscience immediately cornered me. What about the innumerable guys I'd beaten? What about the people I'd killed in Vietnam? And the times I'd lied to my wife and cheated on her? *Surely this man doesn't believe God would forgive all that.*

''You see, God is perfect,'' the speaker continued. ''And in His holiness, He can't have anything to do with us sinners. But He loves us so much that He Himself took the just penalty for all the sins in all our lives.'' *No! This is too good to believe.*

''So God is reaching out to you. He is wanting you to know that in spite of what you may be or in spite of what you may have done—you may have messed up your life completely—God still loves you. He is reaching out to you and inviting you to come and to share that love with Him, no matter how deeply you may have gone into sin. Jesus offers forgiveness to us as a free gift. All we have to do is accept it.''

My eyes burned. My heart pounded. I don't remember laying the rifle down, but I must have discarded it. I was lost in this new message, trying to understand the unfamiliar words. Never before had I heard the good news this man was proclaiming.

''You're not beyond God's love. He's reaching out to you now and He wants to be to you a Father, a loving Father to provide for you all that you may want or need.'' Images of my human father invaded my mind. But this was not the kind of father the speaker was talking about. ''I would encourage you to receive

God's love today. Do you feel guilty about your past? Do you have things in your memory that you wish had never happened? Do you long for forgiveness? If you do, accept it right now! The Bible says, 'The wages of sin is death, but the gift of God is eternal life through Jesus Christ our Lord.' ''

By now tears were pouring down my face. I had slipped off the chair and onto my knees. It had never occurred to me that it was *God's* forgiveness I needed. I had never imagined that *He* could bear the burden of my violent, bitter past.

''All have sinned and come short of the glory of God.'' The baldheaded man smiled a lot as he spoke. He seemed genuinely happy about his message. ''If you think you're the worst sinner on earth, don't worry. There's nothing you could ever do that God can't forgive.''

Nothing! Does this preacher know about guys like me?

''Just ask Him, right now. Ask Jesus to come into your heart, to cleanse you from your past. Accept His free gift of forgiveness. You'll never be the same again.''

This serene, friendly man asked everyone watching him to pray. That was no problem; I was already in the proper praying position. My body was rocking with heavy sobs as he began the prayer, ''Lord Jesus...''

''Lord Jesus...'' I repeated, so choked with emotion that I was unable to speak out loud.

''I'm sorry I'm a sinner. I'm sorry I've broken your laws.''

''Oh God! I'm a sinner...''

''Please come into my life and cleanse me.''

''Lord, *please* come in...''

''I know that I can't do anything to save myself.''

"I can't save myself..." I whispered.

"Thank You for dying on the cross to save me from my own sinful past."

"Thank You...thank You...thank...You..."

I don't know how long I knelt there. My tears poured out like a tidal wave, released from some inner dam, some reservoir of guilt and shame. When at last I became aware again of my surroundings, I realized that at this very moment Sharon was at church! And I knew from my occasional visits that people went "to the altar" when they "got saved." Now I wanted to go up there myself!

I jumped up, rushed into the kitchen, grabbed a towel, wiped my wet face, then raced out the front door to my car. I drove like a madman toward the church. After skidding into a parking place, I slipped in the back door.

The minister was closing the service. My eyes quickly scanned the room for Sharon. She wasn't here. "Is there anyone here who would like to make a public profession of faith tonight?" the preacher asked. "Would you like to let everyone know that you've invited Jesus to live in your heart? Please come forward now while we all sing. Someone will meet you here and pray with you. Let's sing together..." The preacher's tenor voice began singing, "Into my heart, into my heart, come into my heart, Lord Jesus..."

Instantly I was on my way down the aisle. As I walked, practically ran, to the front of the little church, a feeling of joy erupted inside me. Never had I felt this good before. As I knelt at the plain wooden altar, I could hear people softly praying in different languages. A man with a heavy Southern accent read to me from his well-worn Bible. "For God so loved the world that He gave His only begotten Son, that whosoever believeth in Him should not perish but have everlasting life.''

''I know!'' I nodded ecstatically. ''I know!''

Several people laid their hands on me and prayed for me. ''Father,'' a woman entreated, ''Take this young man and cleanse him of all his sins.''

''In Jesus' name we bind the power of Satan in his life,'' said a man with quiet authority. ''Deliver him from any control the enemy may hold over him.''

Suddenly everything I'd ever done wrong seemed to pass before me. In a moment I saw the fights. The Vietnam killings. The immorality. The cruelty to Sharon and the boys. The stealing from the market where I'd once worked. The lies. The bitterness. And most of all, the anger—torrents of anger expressed in shouts, curses, reckless driving, violent actions. And then just as quickly as it came, it was all gone! I was immediately, miraculously freed from all the guilt of all the horrible things I had ever committed.

Then a thought flashed through my mind: *How can I be sure I won't start living the same way all over again?* I began to weep again, feeling a strange new fear. As if he could see into my heart, one of the old gentlemen who knelt with me spoke. ''The Holy Spirit is going to give you the ability to change your ways, son. He's come to live inside you now. He will fill you with the strength you need to live the Christian life.''

The others around us agreed with quiet expressions of ''Praise God'' and ''Hallelujah.''

When the little service finally ended, I walked with great excitement out to the car. *I wish Sharon could have been here,* I thought. *I wish I could have shared this with her.* I pulled the car out into the street and headed home. As I drove I felt clean. I felt loved. I felt the most exceptional peace I could ever have imagined.

I thought about Mamacita. She would understand

what had happened tonight! I remembered how she had prayed for me when I was a little boy in Mexico City. It was in her home that I had experienced peace, but not this peace. No, this was far greater than I had ever dreamed possible. It was indescribable!

At a stoplight, I recalled the 24 years I had wasted. How self-serving I had been! Hate was my source of energy. Now I was being fueled by a powerful new Source—God's Holy Spirit! Why had I never heard of this power before? Or had I been told but simply had not listened?

A toot from the car behind me told me the light was now green. I let the driver pass as my thoughts turned to countless Vietnam veterans who had spent hundreds of hours and thousands of dollars on psychotherapy. So many of my fellow soldiers and marines had literally lost their minds having to deal with all the guilt and horror of that vile war. They were looking for the very thing I had found this night—and my healing had come instantly and free of charge. God had forgiven me in a moment. I was overwhelmed with gratitude. *No shrink in the world can offer this kind of help,* I thought, recalling my own futile experiences in mental therapy. *Only God Himself can give a man a second shot at life.*

And, of course, I thought about Sharon. *She'll be so surprised!* I grinned at the prospect of telling her my miraculous story. Then all at once I shuddered, remembering the deadly plans I had nearly executed just hours before. Had I left the rifle beside the chair? She knew my threats. I had to reach her before she left.

For the second time that night, I steered my sports car into the driveway. I ran to the door—still without my key. I knocked. I could hear activity inside, but no one opened the door. I knocked again. "Sharon, please let me in!" I yelled. "I won't hurt you or the kids. I promise."

I heard the lock turn, and then Sharon opened the door a few inches and peered out at me. "Honey, let me in!" I blurted. "You're not going to believe this—I've been born again!"

She hesitated a moment, looking me dead in the eye with an expression as cold as ice. Then, before I could utter another word, the door slammed soundly in my eager, hopeful face.

10

New Eyes,
New Vision

I couldn't help but chuckle at the absurdity of this situation. Here I stood, overflowing with joy at having finally accepted Christ into my life. But my devoted Christian wife wouldn't let me in the house!

I knocked again. "Sharon! Let me in!"

At last the door opened. Sharon leaned quietly against it. She was unamused, with sadness on her face.

"Baby, listen! I heard a guy on TV. He told me about Jesus. And I asked Him into my life. I'm born again! I really am! Can you believe it?"

"No." Sharon's voice was emotionless. "I'll have to see it to believe it."

"But Sharon...look at me. I'm clean! God's cleaned me up! I'm forgiven. Isn't this what you've always wanted—a Christian husband?"

I moved into the living room and Sharon closed the door behind me. The rifle was gone. The television was off. I immediately headed for the telephone in the kitchen and called Sharon's sister, Shirley, in Santa Cruz, and then her mother. "I'm a Christian!" I told them. "I've been born again!" As I told them what happened, I started to cry for joy as these two women who had prayed for me told me how pleased they were. But Sharon just looked at me, then stared out the window into the night, showing no emotion.

Once I was off the phone I bounced back into the living room. "Raul," she finally said, "it took me all these years to get hard inside . . . to make up my mind to leave you. It took me all these years to give up my convictions about divorce. And now, just when I've finally decided to go, you show up saying you're born again."

"But I *am* born again!" I interrupted.

"Perhaps. I know I can't leave you now. It would be wrong not to give you a chance to prove that what you say is true. But don't expect me to jump up and down with excitement, okay? To tell you the truth, I'm disappointed. I was looking forward to starting my life all over again."

"But we *are* going to start over!" I grabbed her around the waist and tried to pull her to me, but she wiggled out of my grasp.

"Please don't touch me," she said.

"Okay, okay." My high spirits were suddenly dampened, yet her reaction was understandable. It seemed hard to believe that the violent scene with Raul had happened only hours before. "Sharon, I don't blame you. I really don't. But just watch—I'm going to show you that I'm changed. You don't have to love me. Just watch. I'll prove how much I love you."

Early the next morning I jumped out of bed and immediately went looking for Sharon's Bible. I knelt down in my office and read the Bible and prayed. Later in the day, during a break in my schedule, I drove home and vacuumed the house, then cleaned up the dog's messes in the backyard. I suddenly realized that I'd always left any kind of housework to Sharon. Maybe this was one way I could say I loved her. After dinner I spent some time playing with the boys and even helped get them ready for bed.

That night I tried to approach Sharon, but she was still cold. I could not believe how my emotions had deepened toward my wife. But she again told me that she wasn't ready for my affection. "You're okay now," she said. "But you need to pray for me. I'm not okay."

In the past when she wasn't responsive, I would bully her. Now I felt none of those harsh feelings. "Honey, I'll wait. However long it takes, I'll wait. I'm really sorry for how I've hurt you. I promise you, things will be different."

Later in the week I bought my own Bible and spent every spare moment reading it. I couldn't absorb the amazing contents of its pages quickly enough. I got up early and stayed up late. This was not a religion, I discovered; this was a relationship. God was meeting me, and I was getting to know Him. It was so incredible that I prayed constantly, not only for myself but for the people around me. I wanted to tell everyone about my experience.

Among the first people I spoke to was my own family. I drove over to my parents' home and found Dad and Xavier there, drinking beer. When I saw them, I felt a strange new emotion, especially for my father: compassion. The hatred was gone, replaced by a desire to see him know Jesus. "Dad! Xavier! You won't believe what happened to me Sunday night! I've been born again!"

"What the _____ does that mean?" he sneered.

"Dad, I just accepted Jesus Christ as my Lord and Savior. And I love you." I started crying as I told him,

"Dad, I'm now the same person anymore. I don't hate you. I was wondering if you could forgive me for being such a lousy son."

Dad looked at me like I was weird, then laughed to my brother, "What do you think of that? Your brother's trying to get religious on us. Guess we're not good enough for him anymore." As Dad and Xavier made fun of my faith, I realized that they had no idea what had happened to me. *I guess they'll just have to see how my life changes*, I thought.

Friday evening I bought some supplies at the hardware store and began to build a runway for our dog. Sharon had always complained that the backyard was too messy for the kids to play in. By containing the dog, I could solve that problem. While I was working, the phone rang and Sharon yelled that it was for me. It was Tom: "Hey, man, we're having a party!"

"I'll be right over," I said. I grabbed a jacket and told Sharon, "I'll be gone for awhile, babe. See you later." As I jumped in the car I suddenly realized, *She probably expects me to come home bombed and beat up.* But that wasn't the reason I felt I had to go.

"Crazy Raul!" one of the guys yelled as I walked into Tom's home. "Haven't seen you in a while. What's happening, man?"

"Lots," I laughed. "You wouldn't *believe* it!"

As the evening progressed I tried to talk to some of the guys about the new Spirit in my heart. Most of them simply laughed it off as another example of my insanity: "Raul's got another new high." If it wasn't sports I was talking about, it was kung fu, or some fight I'd had, or some chick I'd met. All of this had always been related with the same intense enthusiasm. So now it was Jesus. Big deal.

But at least one person listened. Late that evening

Joe Salaiz, an old buddy from high school, and I had a serious conversation. Joe had quite a reputation. If he wasn't drunk at one party, he was stoned on drugs at another. Like me, he had spent some unpleasant days in Vietnam. And he was quick to talk about his dreary memories.

He got up and shakily poured himself another drink. "I guess you really never leave Nam. Only your body leaves. Your gut stays there forever."

"I know what you mean," I answered, hardly able to control the urge to spill my story all at once. Excitement raced through my body as I thought of the good news I had to share with him.

"Joe, you don't *have* to live like that anymore. I was the same way . . . ghosts always chasing me. But God's cleaned up my life. I asked Jesus Christ into my life, and there's no more guilt—no more fear!"

Sharon and I had already decided to go to Calvary Chapel the next night for the Saturday night concert. "Hey, why don't you come with us, Joe?" I said as the party began to break up. "You'll dig the music. And you can hear some more people explain what I'm trying to tell you."

Sharon was waiting up when I got home, and I could tell she wasn't sure what to expect when I walked through the door. "You won't believe what happened," I blurted out. "I told the guys about how I accepted Jesus. And Joe was really interested. He's going with us to Calvary Chapel tomorrow night!"

Perhaps the words didn't sink in. She didn't seem excited about my news—only relieved that I wasn't drunk. *Maybe she expects this to wear off,* I thought. *I must be patient. She sees this as only another fad. I had promised to change before, but it never lasted.*

The next evening Joe rode silently with us to Costa

Mesa, staring out the window as we drove down the freeway. The closer we got to the church, the more I wondered if inviting him along was such a good idea. *Maybe he's not ready for Christian rock and roll.*

But Joe seemed to relax once the concert started. After the music ended, the emcee asked if anyone wanted to accept Jesus into his heart. Joe practically jumped over us and ran down the aisle. Sharon and I looked at each other in amazement. Later, as he met us at the car, he grinned, "I couldn't wait to get down there. I saw the change in you, Raul. Whatever you had, I wanted it!"

Just about the time I thought everything about the old Raul was gone, Sharon and I had a disagreement. Suddenly the old rage ignited in me and I grabbed her by the neck. "I knew it!" Sharon shrieked. "I knew it wouldn't last."

Stunned by my action, I withdrew my hand, then turned and walked out of the house. Aimlessly I headed down the street. *This can't be!* I cried, tears starting to flow down my face. "God, what's wrong? Why did this happen? I thought You'd changed me. Lord, why did I get angry? Can you ever forgive me? I was wrong to grab Sharon. I don't want to be that way again. That was the old Raul, not the new."

Gradually as I walked, perhaps for an hour or longer, I sensed God lovingly saying, "I forgive you. My Son died for that sin too." And then I walked on, feeling His soothing presence.

Finally I was able to return home, only to find that Sharon was still angry. "Where did you go?" she demanded. "I thought you were a Christian. Why can't you control yourself?"

"I'm sorry, Honey. I took a walk so God could

minister to me. I really blew it, and I'm sorry. It won't happen again.''

But it wasn't that simple. A few days later a driver cut me off on the freeway, then flipped me the bird. Again the old rage flared up. I gunned my car and challenged him to meet me at the next exit. ''Wait!'' Something told me to slow down, to let it pass. But why did I get so angry? Where did that anger come from? ''Lord, I don't want to hurt anyone, but I don't want to be a sissy, either. Do I have to let people push me around?''

I went to the Bible and read in Romans about the conflict between the sin that remains in my flesh and the new Spirit of Christ that dwells within me. I saw that change did not happen instantly. There was a process involved in which I had to recognize that the old sin nature was no longer in charge of my life. It had to be taken to the cross and crucified with Christ. Though sin still acted as though I was its slave, I didn't have to surrender to its desires. But the battle for God's Spirit to have total domination of me would last the rest of my life.

That knowledge helped some, but not when I again found myself reacting to Sharon with a shove or an abusive squeeze. This could not be of God, but how could it change? I never hurt her like before, for I always stopped and took a walk, pouring my heart out to God. This was one area that *had* to change, and soon.

Then one day, right after I'd hurt Sharon again, I was reading my Bible during a break at the kung fu studio. In the book of Acts, Saul was traveling to Damascus to round up Christians and kill them. Suddenly a light from heaven blinded him and he fell to the ground. ''Saul, Saul, why are you persecuting me?'' Saul asked, ''Who art Thou, Lord?''

And God answered, "I am Jesus whom you are persecuting."

There was my answer! I immediately called Sharon, and as she answered I started crying. "Sharon, I want to tell you that I'm *really* sorry for hurting you." She didn't say anything, but I knew she had to be wondering how long she would have to hear that line. "I want you to know that I don't think I will ever hurt you again. I've been reading the Bible, and God said to me, 'Raul, why are you persecuting me?' I've just realized that when I persecute you, I'm persecuting God."

That dramatic moment, about six months after my conversion, was a major turning point. Realizing that when I hurt Sharon I was actually hurting Christ was the motivation I needed to change. I wanted to please God more than anything else. Never again did I physically abuse my wife.

As Christmas drew near, Mamacita arrived from Mexico City for a visit. Joy bubbled inside me as we drove to my parents to see her. "I know she'll understand," I told Sharon. "She's always been close to God."

The years had weathered my grandmother's face considerably since my boyhood. Time had sprinkled gray through her black hair. But tears filled her eyes as we talked. In her expression I could see great peace. A long-ago prayer of hers had been answered, for she knew the instant she saw me that God had transformed my life.

On Sunday night Mamacita attended church with Sharon and me. Since the service was conducted in English, she could understand nothing. I was glad she was with us, but felt sorry she wasn't able to hear the message the pastor was preaching. He concluded,

according to his custom, by asking if anyone would like
to walk forward to receive Christ. Then soft music
began to play. Suddenly, without a word of warning,
Mamacita rose and moved past me to the aisle and
walked down to the altar. How could she have grasped
what the pastor said? After the service concluded, she
made her way back to us, radiantly happy. "I just knew
inside that I *had* to go up there!" she explained in
Spanish. As we talked further, I realized that she had
never before actually invited Jesus Christ to live in her
heart. "I've always believed in Him. I've always prayed
to Him. But tonight I realized that there was something
more I had to do. And so I did it!"

My days, already full of activity, became even more
full as I allowed plenty of time for Bible study and
prayer, and invited friends to our home for a Bible
study. Many times on Saturday night Sharon and I took
friends to the concerts at Calvary Chapel. One night
after the program I saw the familiar face of the man
who had introduced me to Christ on television.
"Sharon!" I whispered, "That guy over there—you see
him? He's the man who led me to Jesus!"

"Raul, that's Chuck Smith. He's the pastor of Calvary
Chapel."

"I don't believe it! I've been coming to his church
and didn't even know it!"

I started collecting the tapes of Chuck's teaching and
played them at the weekly Bible study in our home.
Since I wasn't very familiar with the Bible myself, I
learned as much from the tapes as everyone else.

The people who weighed heaviest on my mind were
my immediate family. My mother started attending
Catholic services more regularly after my conversion,
yet she was even more unhappy. And her relationship
with my father seemed completely hopeless. The time

spent with my parents was unbearably strained. Several angry outbursts still exploded between us.

However, my relationship with Xavier had improved somewhat. In many ways I saw that my brother was like my dad. He too had a drinking problem, and his mouth could spew forth the filthiest language imaginable. At times Sharon and I had to tell him to watch his language in our home, and he had reacted by throwing beer bottles against the house, splattering glass across the lawn. But we had also had close times. Xavier had followed my lead and taken up kung fu. Together we had opened a studio, and we often did demonstrations together. But Dad had always sabotaged our relationship, and six months after our studio had opened, Xavier pulled out, convinced by Dad's accusations that I was cheating him in the business. Xavier opened his own studio and did well, and occasionally we did demonstrations for promotional purposes. This had helped improve our relationship.

Late one night our phone rang and Sharon answered. "Yes. . . yes it is." Her voice sounded frightened. "Yes. Ries. That's right. Yes, his brother is here." She cupped her hand over the receiver as she handed it to me. "It's the Covina Police Department. Something about Xavier."

The businesslike voice on the phone informed me that my brother was in critical condition at the Covina Intercommunity Hospital. "I'll be right down," I said. As I ran out the door I told Sharon, "Pray for him. . .he doesn't know the Lord!"

When I arrived at the hospital, the situation was almost hopeless. The doctor told me that Xavier had been riding his chopper through an intersection. "Some driver ran the light," he said. My brother had been declared dead at the scene of the accident, then revived just enough to be taken to the hospital. Now he lay in a strange twilight between life and death. "Motorcycles—I get about one of these guys a week," the doctor said. "Half of them make it; the other half don't."

Xavier spent the next four weeks in the hospital, and many days I prayed for him by his side. As he grew stronger, I tried to lead him to Jesus. Not surprisingly, he was more open than ever before. Yet something still held him back. "I don't know, Raul," he sighed one afternoon. "I can see the change in you. But I'm not quite ready to give up living. You know what I mean?"

"I know one thing," I answered. "If it weren't for God, you wouldn't *be* living!" I stared at him in amazement, frustrated that he had missed the point. God had obviously saved his life so Xavier could live for Him.

During Xavier's hospitalization, my mother quietly admitted to me that she was growing dissatisfied with her pursuit of a more active Catholic faith. "I keep going to church," she said. "I'm doing everything I'm supposed to do. But nothing is happening on the inside. I feel empty. And Raul, things are getting worse with your father. I'm more afraid of him than ever. One of these days he's going to kill me."

"Mom, you've got to ask Jesus into your heart." One of the verses I'd been memorizing popped into my mind. I carefully quoted it for her. "Jesus said, 'Behold I stand at the door and knock. If any man hear my voice and open the door, I will come in to him and dine with him, and he with me.' Mom, that means Jesus will be with you every minute of the day—not just at church or when you're saying your Rosary. He died on the cross for your sins! *You* don't have to do anything. Just accept His free gift. That's all there is to it."

Mom and I prayed together. But, like Xavier, she

wasn't quite ready to invite the Lord into her life. And once again I talked to Dad. How many times I had invited him to give his life to Jesus, but he would ignore me or curse me or make some sarcastic comment about how "holy" I had become, and how "you and your holy wife think you're so much better than us."

Mom's statement about her frustration with the church bothered me. I thought about how she was displaying statues in her home. She was trying so hard to do the right things. But she was missing the relationship. One afternoon I impulsively drove over to her house. I walked in the front door and said, "These idols have got to come down, Mom!"

Mom was shocked. "But, Raul, they're not idols. I don't pray to them..." Her voice faded as she feebly tried to explain that the statues were "just reminders."

"What do you mean you don't pray to them? Then what are all these candles for? You can't have this stuff around. It's keeping you from knowing Jesus." Then I began to share with her what the Bible says about idols and who Jesus Christ really is.

Over the next few weeks Mom started coming to church with us more frequently. One Sunday after morning service, Sharon asked her, "How come you're not going to Catholic Church so much these days?"

"Well...I've been comparing the two churches in my mind. I feel closer to God when I come here with you. I'm not sure what it is..."

Gently Sharon asked, "Mom, have you asked Jesus to live in your heart?"

There was a moment's pause. I noticed tears welling up in her eyes. Then a warm smile lit up her face as she said, "Yes, I've asked Him into my heart."

Xavier's recovery required a long period of time and the pain stretched his patience to the limit. I could see that this was maturing him emotionally. But how I wanted him to know the Lord! Sharon and I prayed for him constantly, as did Mother and Mamacita.

Finally Xavier was able to resume his kung fu exercises again. His skills returned with surprising speed, and soon we were working out together. One afternoon we were practicing with kung fu sticks at a demonstration in East Los Angeles. Xavier would use his stick to block the blow from mine. We repeated the procedure over and over again. I'd turn, he'd lift his stick, I'd attack, he'd block the blow.

All at once, as I lowered my stick against his, I heard a splintering sound. As if in slow motion, I watched the end of his fractured staff fly up and pierce his eye. Xavier immediately pulled the stick out and clutched the side of his face.

My heart stopped for a moment. My body froze in fear. A sinister fluid seeped between his fingers. In spite of all the fights I'd had and all the killing I'd witnessed, I was trembling uncontrollably. I would have expected to be more hardened, but my new heart wasn't equipped to deal with such a hideous injury. Instinctively I knew that his eye was gone.

I don't know how long I was frozen . . . perhaps only a couple of seconds. I grabbed a towel and stuffed it against his face and we rushed to the hospital. In the emergency room, the doctor confirmed the extent of the injury. What remained of Xavier's eye was eventually removed. Never before had I felt such agony over anything. I would gladly have pulled out my own eye and given it to my brother.

Several hours later, as Xavier woke up from the surgery, I stood by his bed and clutched his hand. He was groggy, but when he recognized me he broke into a big grin. "How are you doing?" I asked.

"You're not going to believe this," he said. "I never felt a thing. There was no pain."

"That's incredible. It was the most horrible sight I've ever seen."

"There's something else I've got to tell you. The instant the stick hit my eye, I *knew* I had to give my life to Jesus Christ. I told Him right then and there that I was His!"

It took a moment for his words to register. Then my tears flowed with joy as I squeezed his hand. Xavier chuckled at my emotion, then said, "Wasn't there a blind man that Jesus once healed? The man said, 'I was blind, but now I see.' "

For Xavier there was no miraculous physical healing. But through the tragedy, he was forever freed from his spiritual darkness. And the glass eye that replaced his ruined one was incredibly realistic. In fact, it is almost impossible to distinguish the real eye from the artificial one.

Gradually, everyone in my family was coming to know the joy of a relationship with Christ. But increasingly I felt a burden for my father. His drinking problem was affecting his health and his marriage, driving mom to the brink of divorce. There seemed no hope for him. . .apart from a miracle.

His Hand Upon Me

11

"For God so loved the world!" I shouted above the noise. A boisterous lunchtime crowd at Baldwin Park High School was having an uproarious time trying to drown out my preaching with catcalls. For the moment, I wondered if I had understood God's message to me. Several weeks earlier I had been in that twilight zone before sleep, praying about how God might use me. Suddenly I sensed a clear message: "Go to Baldwin Park High School and share the gospel." Instantly I was fully alert. Had I imagined those words?

The next day I went down to the school and asked to see the principal. Mr. Gilbert was no longer there, but my reputation still remained. The new principal and the dean of boys promptly called the Baldwin Park Police Department. "You show up again, Ries, and you're in jail," was their message. "You wore out your welcome here a long time ago."

I was slightly discouraged, but the words—I believed they were from God—had been so clear that I felt I couldn't give up easily. A couple of days later I returned, and this time the two administrators allowed me to sit down and tell them what God had done in my life. "I'm *not* the same guy you used to know," I tried to explain. "Jesus has changed me from the inside out. I know the kids here have a lot of problems, and I think what I've learned can help them. All I want is a chance to speak during the lunch hour to anyone who wants to listen."

The two men looked at each other, then reluctantly agreed. "But you're on your own," said the principal. "Don't expect us to look out for you."

With much optimism, I began my noontime Bible study and was greeted by insults and blobs of flying food. I was the new joke on campus, and the kids laughed so hard that I could hardly be heard. "It's a good thing they didn't try that stuff back in the old days," I said to Sharon one night with a grin. "I would have *destroyed* them." In spite of my cold reception, I doggedly returned week after week in obedience to my call.

About this time I faced another major test of my new spirit. My sister Sonia had been married in a civil service when she was 15 years old. Now that she had turned 18, a Catholic wedding was required in order for her to receive the church's blessing. Everyone was invited.

I had a sinking feeling that this was one family event we should skip. "Something's gonna happen, Sharon. We're asking for trouble if we show up."

"Raul, Sonia's your *sister!*" Sharon protested. "We've got to go or she'll never forgive us."

"I know," I sighed. "But believe me, it's not a smart move."

The hour-long Catholic ceremony brought back painful memories. I had shared with my sister and her husband, Gary, about having a personal relationship with Christ. They were going through this ritual only to please my family, not because it held any meaning for them. Why go through this meaningless exercise? As the service drew to a close, I whispered to Sharon, "Let's go home."

A reception was planned at my parents' house. "Let's just go and have a quick piece of cake. Then we'll head home," Sharon promised. Within minutes of our arrival, Dad walked over to Sharon and shoved a glass of champagne into her hand. "No thanks," she said sweetly. Dad knew she didn't drink.

"What do you mean 'No thanks'?" Dad glowered at her. "This is a *wedding*. Can't you even drink a toast to the bride and groom?"

"You know I wish them the best. But I'll pass on the champagne."

I watched this little scene with mounting irritation. No one else had noticed the interchange, but Dad intended to make this a major issue. "Hey, everyone!" he shouted. "Look who won't drink! Can you believe it!" Sharon was already rounding up our boys to head home. Xavier and his wife also recognized our predicament and were preparing to leave.

I tried to quietly intercede. "Come on, Dad...be cool." I could feel anger surging from within, reminding me of those old days when I would have relished this kind of chance to embarrass and even hurt my father.

Dad turned to me and started poking me in the stomach. "You _____ hypocrite!" He spat the words in my face, his alcohol-laden breath stinging my nostrils. "Your wife thinks she's too good to drink a toast to *your* sister. You gonna let her get away with that?"

"Relax, Dad..." I tried to pull away, seeing Sharon

was at the door with the kids and Xavier with Trudy, his wife, ready to leave.

Dad grabbed my shirt. "What are you, some kind of chicken?" By now the room was deathly still. "You too religious to fight me?" he roared.

I turned and headed for the door. Dad followed me and gave me a shove. I pushed him away with my foot. "Did you see that?" he yelled. "Did you see him use that kung fu kick on me? Some Christian you are!"

By now Sharon, the kids, and I were running down the street to our car. Father was running behind us, filling the air with his favorite insults. "You little chicken! You're a hypocrite. Your religion is nothing but a big show. The fact is, you're *afraid* to fight me!"

For the first time in my life I was running away from a fight. In fact, I *was* scared. I was afraid that if I fought him I'd kill him. My emotions were in a turmoil as I jumped into the car. The old anger was fighting my new spirit, but I wasn't going to give it a chance to win.

"Thanks a lot!" I snapped at Sharon as we pulled away, leaving Dad cursing us from the curb. "It's all your fault."

"I'm sorry..." she murmured. "You were right. What a disaster."

I finally calmed down as we arrived home, and I was able to take a walk and talk it out with God. I realized that there was nothing I could have done in that situation except to run. "Oh, Lord," I prayed, "Is there any hope for my father? Won't you bring him to Yourself?"

At least there was plenty of ministry happening to quickly divert my attention from my father. One morning a warm Santa Ana wind blew all the smog out of the valley. It was a gorgeous day and I suggested that Sharon come with me to my weekly time at Baldwin Park High School. "No, you go ahead without me," she said. "I'll be praying for you." I wanted Sharon to participate more in my ministry, but she wasn't ready. Yet she recognized that God's hand was on my life. It was taking her emotions a long time to catch up to the reality of God's work in our lives.

As I arrived in the campus courtyard during the lunch hour, I sensed God saying to me, "Instead of standing on the grass, climb up on one of the benches."

I obeyed and and tried to speak. But I felt at a loss for words. "Lord," I prayed, "You've got to speak through me."

Suddenly I heard myself shout, "Listen up! I used to go to this high school. I've been in a lot of fights. I was always getting in trouble. I'll bet I've been kicked out of this school more times than all of you put together." As I spoke, I sensed that God was directing me to give His message, and it was passing unhindered through my mouth. I wasn't even sure just what I was saying, except I knew that I hadn't prepared it. As I spoke, the usually unruly crowd became absolutely still.

"I met a man who totally changed my life. His name is Jesus. You need to invite Jesus into your lives right now! It takes a real man, a real woman to follow Him. Hey, Jesus was willing to die for you. Are you willing to follow Him, to believe in Him? If you'd like to receive His forgiveness, come up here right now and talk to me. Don't wait another minute."

There was silence...then a gradual rustling. A handful of kids began moving toward me. I couldn't believe my eyes. As the first few kids came, more joined them. Some of them were crying. There were boys and girls holding hands. Athletes. Cheerleaders. Roughnecks. Bookworms. All kinds were coming. As the crowd grew in front of me, I led them in a prayer like the one I'd prayed when I had accepted Jesus Christ as my Lord and Savior. When we were finished, someone told me she had counted 400 teenagers in the throng—about one-fifth of the entire student body!

From that day on, my work at the high school was transformed. Now I could hardly wait to return to teach the Bible to an eager gathering of new converts. We began to pray together, sing together, and share our lives with each other.

The little Bible study that Sharon and I had started in our home, listening to Chuck Smith's tapes, was also growing. After it passed 30 members, we moved it to the kung fu studio. Many of the students from the high school came and brought members of their family. In addition, we would invite them to join us at church on Sunday, but soon there were so many of us that our friends wanted to meet Sunday mornings at the studio.

I had no intention of starting a church. But how could I stop the moving of God's Spirit in these lives? More and more of my time was spent in preaching and teaching the Scriptures. As a result, business at my kung fu studio started to slip. The demonstrations were the first to go, and they had been a primary recruiting tool. Then some students left as I shared my testimony and invited them to stay after the kung fu lessons to learn more about Jesus. They always stayed—they still feared me too much not to—but afterward some didn't return.

The drop in business didn't concern me, though Sharon was not aware of the extent to which our income had suffered. Something within me was saying that kung fu instruction would not be my life's work. Nothing approached the ecstasy I experienced from the kids at school and the people in the studio who met Christ through my witness. I only had to think of Joe, and people like Dave who was always getting loaded.

Joe and I had visited Dave one night and talked for several hours about the Lord. What excitement there was when he prayed to accept Christ and we watched him flush all his drugs down the toilet!

Within months more than 300 people were attending the studies at the studio, and we had to move down the street to the Fox Theater. Then Sharon told me that she was pregnant again. I rejoiced at the news of having a new baby in our home.

Attendance grew even quicker after we moved into the Fox. Chuck Smith came down one evening to speak. After our meeting Sharon and I took him out for dinner, and there I shared with him how God had used him to bring me to Christ. Chuck was enthused about my conversion and the obvious fruit of my witness in the community. "Raul, we're going to have a special one-week intensive Bible school," he said. "Why don't you come down to Costa Mesa for that? It will help you learn even more about the Bible."

I immediately accepted Chuck's invitation and signed up for the "Shepherd's School." That week of full-time study made me realize that the one thing I wanted to do more than anything else was preach the gospel. It motivated me to spend more time learning the Word of God and studying to be an effective communicator. The fact that English was my second language was a problem, and so was my lack of biblical knowledge. Yet God was obviously using me in spite of all the obvious obstacles.

One night during dinner I told Sharon what I was thinking. "The kung fu studio seems to be closing down because I cannot give it the necessary time to keep it up."

Sharon turned pale at the news. "Raul, what about the baby? What are we going to do for an income? No one's paying you to do the ministry."

"Don't worry. God will take care of us. I will get a job to take care of our bills and pay for our baby. Anyway, I'm not worried, as the Lord has always had a job for me."

I met with Chuck Smith shortly afterward. "I was talking to someone from the San Gabriel Valley yesterday," Chuck said. "He told me that we need a Calvary Chapel in that area. You know what I told him?"

"What?" I answered.

"I told him that we've already got one." His smile got bigger as he watched my reaction.

"You mean. . . us!" I jumped up. "I don't believe it! We can call ourselves Calvary Chapel West Covina?"

"That's right." Chuck couldn't help but laugh at my outburst. "And Raul, I want you to prepare for ordination. You've been studying very hard. My staff and I will help you become ordained." My ordination officially occurred on November 28, 1975.

One of the things I had learned from Chuck was that if God was moving in a ministry, He would provide the necessary finances. As yet no one knew of our plans, and I had no intention of making any financial appeal. I did not want to take money from the church, and I'd seen enough already to know that even ministers can mishandle money. But Sharon informed me that the need was real when she came home from her monthly appointment with the pediatrician. "Raul, the hospital requires that we pay *800 dollars* for the baby's delivery—*in advance!* If we don't pay it by the eighth month, I can't have the baby there."

"God will take care of it," I assured her. "Don't sweat it."

To help ease her mind, I took an extra part-time job stocking shelves at a grocery store. We both realized that this was mostly a symbolic gesture, for the five-dollar-an-hour wage would never provide us with the money we needed for the hospital. It seemed ironic that I would work for such small wages when not long before I had earned 300 dollars per hour and more with the studio. But I felt I needed to do whatever I could to provide for my family, and then trust that God would provide whatever else was needed.

One day Sharon rushed into the house with the mail. Her face was flushed with excitement. "Look!" Into my hands she thrust an envelope. "Four hundred dollars!" That would cover half the hospital bill. "The letter says, 'God laid it on our hearts to send you this'!" It had no name on it.

A few weeks later some women in our Bible study had a shower for Sharon. They took up a collection to buy her a special gift, but gathered more than they expected. "We didn't know what to get for you," the hostess said, "so we're giving you the money. You get whatever you need." With a smile she handed Sharon a card. Inside was another check...for 400 dollars!

That night Sharon and I prayed together and thanked God for His provision. Then she looked at me in a new, intense way. "Raul, God has His hand on you. I can see it, just in the miraculous way He's provided this money. And He's using you to reach so many lives. I guess I thought the enthusiasm would wear off after awhile, but it never has. I would be wrong to doubt you any longer."

It was 3½ years after my conversion that Sharon said those special words. How thankful I was that I had allowed her time to see God's work in my life! Now our marriage started growing even stronger, and together we plunged wholeheartedly into the ministry.

The Fox Theater quickly filled up, and Calvary Chapel in West Covina had to start holding two services on Sunday. We used the now-closed studio to provide nursery care during our services. The financial need was still real, but gradually people began providing for us without our asking. One businessman who didn't know our need told me that he felt God was telling him to tithe each month and give the money to the church for my support. Then our board instructed us to begin taking an offering on Sunday mornings, and from that I was put on salary. But the need for space was an ever-increasing problem. Even with two services, the theater soon became cramped.

One day I drove past an old, boarded-up Safeway store and saw a dilapidated "FOR SALE" sign on it. After making inquiries with the appropriate real estate agent, our church miraculously scraped together 1500 dollars for a deposit. We were convinced that God wanted us to have the building, so we decided to apply for a loan. The manager at the bank didn't laugh at us, but his message was explicit: "No credit history, no loan."

I drove down to Costa Mesa to visit with Chuck Smith, who I now considered my pastor. I asked him for his advice regarding the old Safeway store. Acting on that advice, our young church soon had a new home.

Our connection with Chuck Smith led to some very interesting opportunities. One day as we talked, Chuck asked me if I would like to go to Israel with him.

"Me? You've got to be kidding."

"Why not? I think you'll enjoy meeting the Prime Minister of Israel."

Fortunately I had a valid passport. A couple of days later Chuck and I were sitting in the office of one of the world's greatest political leaders—Menachem Begin. As we waited for him to arrive from another meeting, I thought of my childhood in Mexico City and my first

14 years in America. I recalled the hate that had festered unhindered inside me as a teenager and young man. I remembered Vietnam and the horrors there, and then my desperate drive to get ahead. I thought of Sharon and the abuse in our home, and our futile struggle to make a good life. For 24 years my life had added up to nothing but failure.

Now here I sat in Menachem Begin's office! No human effort I might have expended could have put me here. I could barely get on campus at Baldwin Park High School. *God, You blow me away! Everything that has happened since that fateful Sunday night is Your doing.*

And then a moment of sadness dulled this shining moment. *My dad. I wish he could be here, too. He'd be so proud.*

My thoughts were interrupted by the great man's arrival. After he graciously greeted us, we discussed the purpose of our meeting and then engaged in some thought-provoking conversation about the prophetic destiny of Israel. In a few minutes it was over.

When I returned home I tried to share the exciting experience with my parents. "I only wish you could have been there too," I gushed to my dad. "It was incredible!" My father nodded, grunted something, and looked away. *Won't he ever change?* I wondered. *It will be an absolute miracle if he ever does!*

One Saturday night in the fall of 1982, the phone rang. "It's your mom," Sharon whispered as she handed me the receiver.

"Raul...I'm scared..." Mom's voice broke into sobs. "Your father is drunk...and he's hassling me so bad..."

"Where is he now?"

"He fell asleep. But he's so restless...I know he's gonna wake up and...who knows what will happen?"

"Come over here and spend the night with us. I'll try to talk to him tomorrow when he's sober."

After so many years of turmoil, my mother had finally gained enough courage to divorce Dad. Then my father had suffered a heart attack and was told he had to stop drinking if he wanted to live. That event had brought my parents back together, and they had remarried. But Dad's old habits were too hard to break. Soon he was drinking again. And often Mom would escape from Dad's drunken wrath to the peace of our home.

I had lost track of the number of times I'd tried to share the gospel with my father. The only times he had visited our church was on a couple of special occasions when our children were performing. Then he had stood in the back, watched his grandchildren, and slipped out the door.

Sunday morning the three of us and our three boys left for church in a somber mood. That morning I preached from the book of 1 John. I was now systematically teaching through the Bible, book by book, verse by verse. I tried to explain to the congregation what the beloved old apostle John had to say to those friends he addressed as "my little children."

My message concluded with one of my favorite verses of Scripture: "This is the confidence that we have in Him, that if we ask anything according to His will, He hears us. And if we know that He hears us in whatever we ask, we know that we have the petitions that we have desired of Him."

As always, I gave an invitation. "God's will is for you to accept His Son, Jesus Christ. If you ask Him to come into your life, to forgive your sins, to make you a new person, He will do so. You will have what you ask. That is His will. So come forward now and receive Him.

There are counselors up here ready to pray with you and help you."

I closed my eyes and prayed as we waited for those who might want to come forward. Silently I applied that precious promise. *Thank You, Jesus, for keeping Your word. Look how You've answered my prayers for Sharon, for Mamacita, for Xavier, for my mother, for the 400 kids at Baldwin Park High School. Lord, You can also change my dad. I know that is Your will. Thank You for changing me. You forgave me and washed away my past. If You can use me, You can do anything!*

Finally I looked up to pray with those who had come forward. There were several people congregated in front, but my eye caught sight of another man walking down the center aisle. A lump immediately appeared in my throat. The man's head was bowed, and tears were streaming down my face. I was hardly able to pray with those who came forward because I was so broken up.

Then, as the counselors escorted him and several others to the counseling room behind the sanctuary, I announced to the congregation, "That was my dad!" In a spontaneous display of affection the congregation erupted in applause. The "absolute miracle" had finally happened!

12

No More Emptiness

A brisk Santa Ana wind had blown all night, clearing the valley of smog. Fresh, cloudless skies stretched across the San Gabriel mountains, promising a sun-drenched afternoon. As I drove toward my parents' home, I felt a sense of peace. Hopeful anticipation seemed to almost warm me as my car cruised along the familiar Baldwin Park streets.

What a different place Mom and Dad's home had become since they had given their lives to Jesus! I actually enjoyed going there to visit with them and to exchange ideas. *It really is a miracle...* I thought to myself as I parked in front of their house.

Walking through the doorway, my eyes quickly moved around the living room, absorbing the various articles that decorated the place. Pictures. Lamps and books. Knickknacks from Mexico. Most of them had been around as long as I could remember. My mind raced back to the day when in my newborn Christian zeal I had destroyed the Catholic icons that had once shared the surroundings. *It was a crazy thing to do,* I smiled silently, *but I'm glad I did it.*

"Oh, hi, Raul. Want a Coke?" Mom automatically headed for the refrigerator.

"Sure. Where's Dad?"

"He'll be back in a minute. He went out to the store."

I followed her into the kitchen. "Hey, Mom, what did you think the day I ripped down all the saints. Were you upset?"

"Well, I wasn't really upset. I just didn't understand why you did it. They were always in our house, and I thought since you were getting more religious, you'd like them more. Instead, you wanted to get rid of them. But I haven't really missed them that much."

"Do you understand now why I did it?"

"I guess you thought we prayed to them or something . . ."

"A lot of Catholic people do, you know, Mom."

"Is that so bad, Raul? After all, it's better to pray to somebody than not to pray at all!"

"No, Mom, that's not really true. Unless you pray to God through Jesus, you aren't really praying at all. Those 'saints' aren't any more important to God than you are!"

"Raul! Don't say that!" Mom's frown reflected her disbelief. "Those saints are great people to the church—not ordinary people like me!"

"Mom, the Bible says we're *all* saints!" Now she put her hand to her forehead in horror. I couldn't help but laugh at her shock. She couldn't imagine herself as a saint. And she certainly couldn't picture *me* being one!

I grabbed the Bible off the shelf and turned to the New Testament book of Ephesians. "Listen, Mom. 'Paul, an apostle of Jesus Christ by the will of God, to the *saints* who are at Ephesus, and the faithful in Christ Jesus . . .' Do you know what that word 'saint' means?

It means 'set apart. Sacred. Blameless. Consecrated.' And that's what we all become when Jesus forgives our sins and saves us.''

''But the saints were chosen by the church for doing miraculous things...'' She looked at me skeptically. ''Shouldn't we respect them for that?''

''We are all capable of doing miraculous things, Mom. You could raise the dead if God wanted you to. So could I. We could *all* see visions. We could *all* heal the sick. We could *all* change the history of the world—through the power of God in us.''

Mom sipped her tea and looked out the window. She was having a hard time absorbing my words. I was contradicting everything she had ever been taught, and yet she could sense the truth in what I was saying. Finally she spoke. ''Well, I can see what you mean. And I don't pray to them, Raul. Not anymore.''

''Mom, that's the most important point of all! The Bible says there is only one Person who can talk to God for us—and that one Person is Jesus. He's called our 'Mediator.' So when we pray to anyone else, we remove Jesus from His proper place. Worse yet, the Bible also says we shouldn't make statues or 'graven images' to use for worship. People who use sacred icons are really breaking the law of God!''

About that time Dad's car turned into the driveway. Mom jumped up to make him a cup of coffee. He walked in with a bag of groceries in one hand and the mail in the other. ''Looks like my mother's going to be here next weekend,'' he said, tossing a letter on the table.

''Mamacita's coming? Hey, that's great, man!'' As always, a visit with Mamacita was something pleasant to anticipate.

Dad sank heavily into his chair, ready to relax. Mom

handed him a steaming cup of coffee and sat down herself, savoring fresh tea. I looked at the scene with quiet pleasure. How many times had the three of us sat together and actually enjoyed each other's company? In my lifetime it had only been possible since God's healing hand had touched my family.

"Raul's telling me about the saints . . ."

"What about them?" Dad's voice sounded a little gruff.

"Well, it was Jesus who changed your life, Dad. Not one of the saints."

He seemed to relax a little. "Yeah, it was. And man, did I ever need changing, too. It's just hard sometimes to admit that the religion you've always had in your family isn't as good as you thought it was. Or at least it didn't do the job somehow. It's hard 'cause we've always been Catholic . . ."

Dad's voice trailed off into thoughtfulness. I couldn't help but sympathize with his puzzled feelings. Of course Jesus Christ was a very important part of the Catholic religion. He was the Savior who died on the cross for everyone's sins. He was raised from the dead and was now in heaven. Those facts were just as dear to Catholic doctrine as they were to me. And yet . . .

"Dad, the problem is, you can't get forgiveness from a *religious system*. You have to be forgiven by *Jesus*. You know there is so much ritual and human effort involved in Catholicism that a lot of people miss the point. They never learn to know God. And even more often they never learn that He really, really loves them!"

"Yeah," Dad laughed, "I was never even sure there was a God . . . much less a God that loved me."

I laughed a little too. "The God I grew up hearing about sure wasn't a God of love. No way. There was a lot of fear. And the more I did wrong, the more I wanted to run from Him. I figured He was gonna nail me! I still can't believe how much He loves me. I just can't believe it.'' My eyes stung with tears for a moment.

Dad nodded silently, prompting me to continue. ''That's the incredible thing. We all needed to cut through the religious stuff and get to know the One who made us . . . and loves us . . . and died on the cross for us. That's it. That's the whole story—accepting His forgiveness and walking with Him. It just blows my mind.''

''We've all got a lot to be thankful for, that's for sure, Raul.''

''Hey, Dad, I got a surprise for you. How would you like to go to South America?''

''What?''

I had to laugh at the shock on Dad's face. ''Yeah! Our church is helping build a church and a Bible School in Colombia. Why don't you come with me? Sharon's Dad is coming, too. We'll have a great time.''

Mom reached over and grabbed Dad's hand. ''Why don't you go? You have the time now.''

''I'll think about it,'' said Dad.

I checked my watch. ''I gotta get out of here. Hey, wait till you hear my sermon tomorrow—it's about the same thing we've been talking about.''

''Saints?'' My mom looked worried.

''One in particular, Mom. Mary.''

''The Blessed Virgin?'' Now she really looked worried.

''Mary, Jesus' mother. See you at church?'' I rushed out the door, waving as I went. *I wonder if they'll show up,* I thought as I drove away.

For several weeks I had been preaching on the difference between religion and a relationship with God. It wasn't just Catholicism that got people offtrack. The same thing could happen at Calvary Chapel, and it could affect even the most sincere Christian. The moment human activity and the cares of this world get in the way of sitting at the feet of Jesus, we lose touch with Him!

But the matter of praying to the Virgin Mary particularly disturbed me. Ever since my own conversion, I had felt that it was a dangerous doctrine. Driving over to my office, I reviewed it again in my mind. *It's the paganism that freaks me out. Every false religious system in the history of the world has had a mother goddess. And you can't escape the fact that a lot of Roman Catholics really do worship Mary. No matter what they tell you, they truly adore her.*

My mind knew what needed to be said. Many of those who came to hear me preach were from Catholic backgrounds. And I wanted them to know the truth from the Scripture. My only dilemma lay in not wanting to offend. Just as with my folks, these sincere people were in love with a tradition. They had more trouble with their own emotional reactions than with actual spiritual truth. Could I speak the truth in love?

Sunday morning I was still grappling with the message. Yet I knew it had to be given. "God," I prayed as I made my way to the church, "You speak through me by the power of your Holy Spirit. Guard my tongue, and yet give me boldness."

And so I preached. I describe the times Jesus made a point of letting Mary know that He was God's Son, with responsibilities that went beyond her scope of influence. "When Jesus was only 12 years old, and Mary was looking for Him in the Jerusalem temple, He said, 'How is it that you sought me? Did you not know that I must be about my Father's business?'

"When Jesus performed His first miracle at Cana, changing the water into wine, Mary was the one who brought the problem to His attention. 'Woman,' He said to her, 'What do I have to do with you?'

"When Mary and Jesus' brothers came to see Him one day, He said, 'My mother and my brothers are these who hear the word of God and do it.'

"It was only from the cross that Jesus gave special recognition to Mary, acknowledging her as His earthly mother. And at that point He gave her over to the care of His disciple John."

Then I went on to tell about the last time Mary is mentioned in Scripture, in Acts 1:13,14. "Who was in the upper room? All the disciples and the women, including Mary—His mother. Was anybody praying to Mary? No! They were praying for the power of the Holy Spirit to fall, as Jesus had promised. And she was praying right along with the rest of them. She knew she needed power as much as anyone there!

"First Timothy 2:5 says, 'There is one God and one Mediator between God and men,' and that is the woman Mary. Is that what it says? No! It says there is one Mediator between God and men, and it is the man Christ Jesus, who gave His life a ransom for all.

"We are *never* to pray to Mary. We are to go directly to the throne of grace through Jesus Christ. We have nothing in Mary. We have nothing in the apostles. But we have direct access to the God of the universe through His only begotten Son, Jesus Christ!"

I stopped for a moment to catch my breath. My eyes moved across the congregation. No one stirred. My heart ached for every person there to understand. I could feel my voice soften.

"I am not against Catholic people. I'm *for* Catholic people because the word "catholic" means *universal—*

one body. I want to let you know that to be a Catholic, a true Catholic, you need to be born again of the Holy Spirit. You need to accept Jesus as Lord and Savior. Then you are one with Him. And then we can all be one with each other."

Several people gave their lives to Jesus after the service, and I was thankful for that. Yet I still felt that there was more to be said on the subject of religion versus relationship. So when Mamacita arrived the following weekend, I was eager to talk to her about what God had done in her life.

Sharon and I picked her up at my folks' place on a cool, clear evening. It was one of those California nights when the palm trees were silhouetted against a deep blue sky. A single star shone through the twilight. We couldn't help but notice the beauty of God's world as we headed for a quiet dinner together.

After we had ordered our food and caught up on some family news, I began to ask the questions that had been spinning around in my mind for days. "Mamacita, after all the time you spent as a Catholic, what made you give your life to Jesus?"

She looked at me for a moment without speaking, putting her answer together carefully. "Raul, a few years ago I went to Mass and sat down in my usual place in the front row—you remember where I always sat."

My memory instantly resurrected a picture of the familiar church of my youth in Mexico City. I could almost smell the incense.

She continued her story: "I was waiting for the service to begin, saying a few prayers, when one of the church leaders came up to me and asked me to move. At first I didn't understand. But then I saw what was happening."

Mamacita paused, took a few bites, and then went on. "A very wealthy couple had come to church. I recognized them immediately. They were prominent people in the community who rarely showed up at Mass. But because of their wealth and position, the priests had decided they should have a seat up in front. Naturally I got out of the way. And I stood in the back for the rest of the service."

Sharon and I looked at each other. How easy it is for people to cater to the wealthy, even in Protestant churches!

"What did that mean to you, Mamacita?"

"Well, it just seemed to sum up my whole situation. This was a perfect example of the emptiness of my religion. Nobody cared about me in that situation. Nobody thought about my feelings. The only concern was for the money and prestige the church might receive through those rich people."

"So what did you do?"

Mamacita smiled. Her next statement took me by surprise. "I started reading the Bible after that. I wanted to know more about God. I knew He wasn't the reason for all the emptiness. I'd always believed in Him. Remember how I used to pray for you?"

I nodded. I remembered very well.

"Well, I learned more at one sitting while reading the Bible than I had learned my entire life attending Mass! I immediately started changing inside. And then, when I had come here and seen the change in your life, I started *seeing* what I'd been feeling and reading. The same life I had been experiencing was evident in you and in the people that were in your church. I finally understood that I could know God personally without any religion at all. And then God showed me that He loved me. After that I was never the same again!"

"But what happened?"

Mamacita smiled, and tears welled up in her eyes. "I asked Him to forgive me and to come into my life. I accepted His free gift of salvation through Jesus. Don't you remember the night I went up to the front of the church to pray?"

Sharon and I nodded. Neither of us would ever forget.

"Well, after that there was no more emptiness!"

No more emptiness. When I returned home that night I fell to my knees in prayer. Could I ever really communicate the bubbling-over fullness of spirit that Jesus gives? Could I ever put into words the overflowing joy and peace that comes when His Holy Spirit transforms a life with love? Could I ever speak well enough to help people clear away the murky residue of tradition and become clean, empty vessels ready to be filled with new life?

"Oh, God!" My prayer poured out in torrents. "You know where I've been. You know where my family has been. And there are millions of others out there locked in the same guilt, the same fear, and the same emptiness as we were. God, You've delivered every one of us. Now use us. Use *me*, Lord. I want to spread the message of salvation to everyone in bondage. Catholics. Protestants. Atheists. I don't care where they're coming from. I want to tell everybody, God. *Everybody!*"

A few weeks later Dad and I were flying to Colombia to tell people there about God's love. Along with a team from our West Covina church, we worked hard all day, then held services at night. For ten days Dad and I enjoyed barbecues, took walks, laughed, cried, and shared. It was like God had restored the father-son relationship we had missed when I was a boy.

As we flew home, I asked Dad what he thought about

138 • *From Fury To Freedom*

the time. "The people were so nice," he said. "It was like they'd known us for years. Does that always happen among Christians?"

"Yes, Dad, at least that's the way it should happen."

"And the way people came every night for the services...Raul, anytime you want me to go with you in your ministry, just let me know."

I couldn't help smiling. God had done far more than bring my father to Christ; He had given him a heart for ministry, too. And now everyone in our family was serving God!

13

From Fury To Freedom

The salt air blew against my wet face, cool and refreshing. I hadn't had time to surf for months, and it felt wonderful to be out on the water again. There at Huntington Beach, under the warm sun, I was waiting for a "big one" to carry me toward the wide, warm sand.

After an hour or so, as I made my way back onto the beach, I glanced at a young man who seemed to be watching me. He sat almost immobile on a towel, his long hair brushing against his shoulders. It didn't take me long to notice that both of his legs were missing. *Vietnam vet, I'll bet,* I thought to myself.

But a closer look revealed that this wary-eyed individual was no stranger. "John!" I shouted as I suddenly recognized him. We had gone through boot camp together. "I can't believe it, man! What are you doing?"

"I'm sure not surfing," he said bitterly, motioning toward his lower body.

"Did that happen in Nam?"

"Where else?" He laughed, but there was no humor on his face.

"Yeah, man. I spent a year there myself. I know what you mean." Pictures flashed into my mind. The explosion of booby traps. The crackle of gunfire. The moaning bodies of friends, lying bloodied and ruined on the ground. Though the nightmares had ceased about four years after my conversion, the memories would never be lost. I hadn't been there when John lost his legs, but I knew exactly what had happened.

"Looks like you came out okay." John checked me out as he spoke. "You always were crazy. What'd you do, kill everybody you saw?"

"Just about. . . I was pretty angry, all right. It didn't take me long to learn to get high on killing. It was like deer hunting or something. You know?"

"Not really. I was only over there two weeks when I got blown away. I didn't have much time for fun." John's brown eyes glinted with rage every time he spoke. He remembered me from boot camp, and hadn't seen me since I gave my life to Jesus Christ. I breathed a quick prayer as I sat down in the sand next to him: *God, open the door for me to witness.*

There was a break in the conversation as a set of enormous waves sent the remaining surfers careening through tufts of spray. Everyone on the beach stopped talking to watch and smile at the excitement. Finally John spoke again. "What are you doing for a living nowadays?"

"I'm a Bible teacher, man."

John looked absolutely stunned. At first he was speechless, then he laughed. "You're kidding, right?"

"No, I'm serious. Ever heard of Calvary Chapel West Covina?"

"I guess so. . . ."

"That's my church, man. I'm the pastor there."

"I never thought *you'd* end up doing that! You're the last person I'd ever have expected to see as a preacher!" John looked at me suspiciously, but his curiosity got the best of him. "How'd you get so religious, anyway?"

"Well, I guess it was because of Nam, really. I was so full of hate before, you know. Remember how I was always getting into fights?"

John chuckled. "Who could forget?"

"When I got over there, I just exploded. I was obsessed with rage. I wanted to kill everybody—including my commanding officers! They finally threw me into a mental hospital, I was so bizarre..."

"You really were crazy!" John grinned at his little joke.

"I was. And then the flashbacks started. And the nightmares. I was never safe from the guilt or the violence. I'd go to sleep upset and wake up in the middle of the night screaming."

"Yeah, me too. I think a lot of guys go through that...I've talked to dozens of vets that have the same problem. Most of them are seeing shrinks trying to get their brains unscrambled."

I took a deep breath. "Well, I got my brain unscrambled in one night. I was so angry I was sitting in my living room with a .22 rifle, waiting to kill my wife and kids. About that time a TV preacher started talking about Jesus Christ. He said that because Jesus had died on the cross for my sins I could be forgiven for every bad thing I'd ever done. *Everything!* I couldn't believe it! I got down on my knees like a prisoner, all chained up in anger and fury. And I got back up on my feet a free man!"

John looked at me sharply, a steely hardness gleaming in his eyes. "Yeah, well I'm not too interested in a God that let *this* happen to me." John pointed to the stumps that once had been strong, healthy legs. "I mean, come on, man, you trying to tell me a God of love would let me get blown away?"

A thousand thoughts raced through my mind. Easy answers would never satisfy a man like John. He was so resentful, so deeply disappointed by life. What could I say? I breathed another prayer: *God, give me wisdom!*

"Jesus suffered too, man. He died on a cross in worse pain than even you felt, as bad as it was. And you know why He died?"

"Yeah...because of politics. He was a victim."

"No way, man. Jesus gave up His life freely. He was the Son of God. He came to this earth for one reason—to die. And He died for you, John. He died so that you could have eternal life. He knows about your pain— He was hurt even worse than you. And He went through it all so you could have eternal life in heaven."

John turned his head toward the roaring sea, thinking about my words. Finally he shrugged. "I still say a God of love wouldn't have let it happen..." Somehow, though, the edge had gone out of his voice.

"Why don't you come by the church and see me sometime. We'll talk some more. I'll buy you lunch. Okay?"

I got up to leave, and offered him my hand. He shook it and grinned. "I never thought you'd turn out to be a preacher, Raul. Yeah, I'll come by sometime. See you around, man."

As I drove home, I thought about John. How many guys like him were still fighting the Vietnam war in their pain-scarred hearts? *There must be thousands and thousands of them. So many amputees. So many guys who still feel guilty for killing when they didn't have any choice.*

One thing I was sure about: People like John don't

understand God's love. They have no idea that God treasures them, that He wants to bless them with kindness and tender mercies. I remembered the night I first understood God's love myself.

I had been studying my Bible, getting ready to teach a lesson from the thirteenth chapter of John's gospel. Verse 5 said, "After that He poured water into a basin, and began to wash the disciples' feet, and to wipe them with the towel with which He was girded."

Washing their feet? I had thought to myself. *This was the God of the universe. How could He do such a humble thing?*

I had read further, discovering that Simon Peter had already expressed my objection: "Lord, do You wash my feet?... You shall never wash my feet!"

Jesus answered him, "If I do not wash you, you have no part with me."

Simon Peter replied, "Lord, not my feet only, but also my hands and my head!"

I could still feel the tears that had stung my eyes the first time those words reached my heart. Jesus loved us enough to wash our feet! Jesus loved Raul Ries enough to wash *his* feet! The immeasurable passion of God for His people became a personal reality to me in that moment.

But what about John? How could I help him understand?

I thought often about my own experiences in Vietnam in the days that followed my "chance" meeting with John. I thought about the surging anger that had been such a part of my personality for my young adult life. The festering sore of rage had never healed. And by the time I left Vietnam, it was hideously infected with hate.

"Satan sure had a hold on you!" a new convert once

remarked after hearing my testimony. I was never sure how much of my rage was from the devil, but it was obvious that I had been totally under the influence of evil when God got hold of me. He met me where my need was greatest. Once He touched me with the warm, healing oil of His Holy Spirit, my inner man was restored to a health I had never known before.

Driving through a spring rain on my way to church one Saturday morning, I was puzzling over the Vietnam veterans' dilemma again. *Maybe it's a matter of forgiveness. . . forgiveness has to start somewhere, though. Where does it begin?*

I had some studying to do, and planned to use some books I had left in my office. I was lost in sermon preparation that rainy day when a soft tap on the door distracted my attention. I looked up, and there was John! It had been weeks since our first encounter, but he had finally made his way over to church. "Hey, man! It's so neat to see you again!" I greeted him. "How are you?"

"If you really want to know, I'm sick of living." John spat out the words. "I'm tired of dragging this screwed-up body around. Sometimes I feel like blowing my brains out."

I looked at the young man and my heart felt like it would break. "John, you've got to meet Jesus. That's all there is to it. You can't go on without Him. . ."

The same hardness I'd first seen at the beach tightened his face again. "God is nobody I want to meet. . ."

Forgiveness. . . it has to start somewhere. "John, do you think this happened to you because God was punishing you for something?"

"Yeah! I had some pretty good times before, if you know what I mean. I guess I had a little more fun than God wanted me to. So He took care of that!"

A bitter laugh ended his outburst.

"So you think God blew off your legs because you were bad? That's just not true, John. God brings us to Himself with kindness, not with anger." I opened my Bible to the second chapter of Romans.

"Do you despise the riches of His kindness and forbearance and longsuffering, not knowing that the kindness of God leads you to repentance?"

John gave me a blank look. What was he thinking?

"It's a lousy world, John. Kids are starving. Innocent people get shot in the streets. Everywhere you look there's tragedy. It's not just you—it's everywhere. And the reason for it isn't God—it's man. Man is full of sin. He's an evil creature, apart from God. And the farther we run from God, the more we contribute to the problem.

"But God has made a way for man to overcome evil with good—through the blood of His Son, Jesus. With His Spirit in your heart, you can start to change the world. You can make a difference. But without Him, you and I are just part of the insanity. You *know* how insane I was, man. That's no secret. But God changed me into a valuable person. He'll do the same thing for you if you'll let Him!"

"You've got to be kidding! How can I be valuable with no legs? I can't do anything now. I'm handicapped. What do you mean 'valuable'?"

"It's your insides that count, John—not your legs and not your arms. It's the person on the inside that God's looking at. He can make your life into something beautiful—legs or no legs! But not unless you let Him change your heart. Why don't you accept His forgiveness right now?"

"Forgiveness for what? For being a cripple?" The searing anger in John's spirit crept into every word he spoke.

"The Bible says, 'All have sinned and come short of the glory of God.' You. Me. Everybody. Even little kids, man. We're all dirty on the inside. And He wants to make us clean."

"So what am I supposed to do?" In all his helplessness, a flicker of hope seemed to register in John's expression. "I'll try anything. I'm so messed up, what have I got to lose?"

"John, I want you to pray with me. Just say the same words I say...God, I'm a sinner."

"God, I'm a sinner..."

"I want so much to be forgiven..."

"I want to be forgiven..."

"I want to ask your Son, Jesus, into my life so I can be changed on the inside..."

And so it was that John accepted Jesus into his tragic life. His eyes were full of light from the moment we finished our prayer. Some changes came quickly, but other things took time. He had a lot of pain to overcome and a lot of forgiving to do.

In the weeks to come, I saw him from time to time at church. I noticed that he was taking better care of himself. His clothes were cleaner. It looked like he was washing his long hair more frequently. But one Sunday I could see at a glance that things weren't right with John. "Hey, man! What's happening? You looked bummed out—what's the problem?"

"Forget it, Raul. It's nothing."

"What do you mean, it's nothing? Are you mad at somebody? Did I say something that upset you?" My mind raced through my sermon, trying to recall anything that might have disturbed him.

"No, it's just...I don't really know if all this stuff is true. I mean, I come here and everybody's talking about God and Jesus and all that. But outside of this place the world goes right on. Nothing's really changed. I don't know anymore what's real and what isn't.''

''Are you reading the Bible, John? Are you in the Word? You've got to stay in the Word, man, or you're gonna fall away...''

''Yeah, I try to read it. But most of it is pretty hard to understand. I know what the words mean, but what does it have to do with me?''

''Are you in a Bible study group?''

''Not really...I went to one, but I didn't know anybody...''

Of course nothing can ever take the place of private Bible study and prayer. Getting personally acquainted with Jesus is one of the most beautiful experiences any new Christian can have. But it was easy to see that John needed fellowship and support from other believers to strengthen his faith. After talking to some of the home Bible study teachers, we found a young man to disciple John, to teach him the Word, to pray with him, to keep track of his needs. Before long John was reaching out himself, learning to help others!

A few months later John and I had lunch. As we sat in a colorful Mexican restaurant near the church, I took a long, hard look at him—and I couldn't help but smile. He was clearly a changed man. ''You don't seem like the same guy I met at the beach. How do you feel about life now?''

''Raul, I'm *not* the same guy. Oh, yeah, I'm still a cripple; you can see that all right. But on the inside I'm at peace. No more nightmares. No more hate. No more bitterness. It's so amazing. I tried to change all that myself, and I couldn't do it. But now God's got hold of me, and I can never go back. Never! I'm a new person!''

''I know, John. The Bible says, 'If any man is in Christ, he is a new creation; old things have passed away; behold, all things have become new.' That's what being born again is all about. You really are a new baby in the Spirit. And when you start being fed the milk of the Word—the Bible—and start resting in God, you grow. You'll get stronger and stronger, John. You can grow into a great man of God."

John looked at me, nodding quietly for a moment. Then he smiled. "There's something I've wanted to ask you for awhile. Do you think demons made us hate? Was all that fury from the devil, or was it just us?"

"Well, there's no way Satan didn't have us in complete control. I know that's true. And I'm sure demons could get us to do just about anything. When you're living in the flesh like we were, you're part of Satan's household. But when God adopted us into His kingdom, Satan had to let us go."

"So we don't have to worry about him anymore . . ."

"That's not what I said, man!" I started to laugh. "He's always prowling around looking for somebody to chew up. What I said was that we don't *belong* to him anymore. And as long as we keep close to Jesus, listen to His voice, read His Word, and obey the directions of the Holy Spirit, Satan's not going to get anywhere with us. He may fight with us, but he can't win!"

"I learned a verse at our Bible study, Raul. It says, 'We are more than conquerors through Him who loved us!' I may be a loser in this world's eyes, but God has made me a conqueror in the Spirit." John's eyes shined with a beautiful joy as he spoke. His face had softened. "God really loves us, Raul. I understand that now. He really, really loves *me*."

My eyes burned with tears as I looked at my reborn friend. "That's neat, John. Only God could have made such a change in you. It's so neat it blows my mind!"

14

Made Complete...
In Him

Autumn winds had pressed a heavy fog against the San Gabriel foothills. Headlights were distorted in the mist, glowing like strange white orbs. I was glad to get home—it was no night for driving.

As I arrived at the house, I noticed that a light was on in the living room. *Maybe Sharon's still up,* I thought. It had been a long evening at the church, and I was exhausted, yet a few minutes with Sharon would help me unwind. Quietly I used my key to let myself in the front door. Sharon looked up and smiled at me as I entered the living room. She was curled up in her favorite chair, her Bible open in her lap. *How many times have I come into the house and found her in that same place, reading God's Word?* I was touched by the scene.

"How'd it go, Raul?"

"Oh, fine...everything's fine." I flopped down on the couch and studied her for a moment. "You know, I can't believe it. I was just thinking that I've come home and found you sitting there reading your Bible

about a million times. And there you are again! Same
robe, same chair, same lamp..."

Sharon laughed. "It used to really make you mad,
didn't it?"

"Oh, yeah...I hated it. It convicted me so much
about my life. Now it blesses me. I still wonder how
you ever survived all those lousy years."

"Sometimes I wonder myself. I sure wouldn't want
to go back. But you know, I think a lot of it was because
of my family. My parents brought me up to turn to the
Bible for help...to seek the Lord, to read His Word."

"So you think you would have divorced me if you'd
come from a different background?" I tried to imagine life without Sharon. It was impossible.

"Oh, probably. But I was always conditioned to
believe that divorce was wrong, and that you shouldn't
run away from your problems. It was ingrained in me
all my life."

A well-worn Scripture came into my mind, and I
quoted it: "Train up a child in the way he should go,
and when he is old, he won't depart from it.' It just
shows you God's faithfulness, doesn't it?"

"That's exactly right, Raul. I'm just so thankful for
the foundation my parents laid in my life. Because of
them, I've always had God's truth as an anchor. And
it's kept me steady when everything else was slipping
away."

I thought about several different wives who had come
to me for counseling the past few months. Some of them
had been physically abused by their husbands. "What
would you say to a woman whose husband beats her
up? I had a lady in my office the other day who was
really scared; she thought her husband would kill her
if she stayed. Why didn't you leave me?"

"I didn't leave you because I didn't want our kids

to end up with a different father. I knew I'd eventually meet somebody else, and that would be the end of it. And I didn't want that to happen. If it had just been me, I think I might have taken off, but I couldn't do that to our boys.''

''But weren't you afraid? Nobody knew better than you how crazy I could get when I was mad.''

''Sure I was afraid. That's why I was packed up and ready to go the night you got saved. I was afraid for myself and I was afraid for our kids. You know, Raul, I would never tell a woman to stay in a house where a man was abusive. But I wouldn't tell her to run out and get a divorce the first time her husband pushed her around, either. Every situation is different. And women with that kind of problem need to listen to God, not to other people.''

''What was God telling you, Sharon?''

''Raul, I don't even know if I've ever told you this before. The night before our wedding, I was so terrified I didn't know what to do. Although I loved you, I knew I was about to be married to a non-Christian, and I knew this could never be God's will. All I could think about was the Scripture that says 'What communion does the temple of God have with Belial?' ''

''And I was Belial?'' I couldn't help but laugh.

''Well, yeah.'' She laughed too. ''I guess you were! Anyway, I just went to the Lord and poured my heart out to Him that night. 'God,' I told Him, 'I've completely blown it. I've got to marry this guy, and I'm so scared. Please help me!' After that I felt a little better, but the real answer came the next day.''

''What happened then?''

''I was still afraid when I woke up the next morning. When I went to the church, and marched down the aisle, I hardly saw you. When we repeated our

vows, I said them to God. I promised to be faithful to
Him, to love and obey *Him* for the rest of my life. It
was like I was marrying the Lord. Then, when the pastor presented us to the congregation, I felt the Holy
Spirit touch my heart and say, 'I have my hand on you.
It's going to be all right!' It was like God was saying,
'Yes, you blew it, Sharon, but I can fix it.' "

"You actually heard a voice?"

"No, not an audible voice, but I understood perfectly
well that God was speaking to me. All my Christian
life I'd walked by faith, believing the Bible. That was
the first time He had ever broken through to me and
allowed me to feel His touch. I knew exactly what He
was saying, and I began weeping for joy."

"I remember that! Now it makes sense. I had no idea
what was going on inside you, but I'll never forget how
beautiful and radiant you looked at that moment. So
that's what was happening! It just shows how God
speaks to us in so many different ways."

"Yes, He does. And that's what made me stay with
you all those years. When God gives us a promise, and
we know it's from Him, He has to keep it. There's nothing more certain in the entire universe."

"That's Isaiah 55:10,11! Listen to this!" I grabbed
Sharon's Bible off her lap and read the ancient, wonderful words out loud.

> As the rain and the snow come down from
>   heaven,
> and do not return to it without watering the
>   earth
> and making it bud and flourish,
> so that it yields seed to the sower and bread
>   to the eater,
> so is my word that goes out from my mouth:

It will not return to me empty,
but will accomplish what I desire
and achieve the purpose for which I sent
   it (NIV).

"That's it!" Joy filled Sharon's voice. "That's the promise that kept me going, Raul. I knew that in God's time and in His way He would make everything right. And He kept His word to me. He really did!"

The next morning the phone rang. I answered it.

"Oh, hi, Raul. This is Mary. Is Sharon there?"

"Sure, Mary, hang on a minute."

I gave Sharon the phone, poured myself some cereal, and sat down to eat breakfast. Sharon picked up the phone and began talking to her friend. I could tell from what she was saying that Mary was having problems with her husband—again.

"Oh, I'm sorry to hear that. I know how hard it is for you, believe me. I've been there. Well, you know, too. You've heard Raul's testimony."

She listened for a moment, then answered emphatically.

"Mary, I didn't get Raul saved! God did!"

There was a pause while Mary spoke. Then Sharon went on. "Sure I prayed for him. And I stuck with him. But my life wasn't dependent on Raul's getting saved. I had to go on and walk with the Lord no matter what."

Again a pause.

"Let me get my Bible, Mary. I want to read you something."

Sharon laid the phone down momentarily. When she returned, she read to Mary Isaiah 54:4-6:

"Fear not, for you will not be put to shame;

Neither feel humiliated, for you will not be
   disgraced. . . .
For your husband is your Maker,
Whose name is the Lord of Hosts. . . .
For the Lord has called you,
Like a wife forsaken and grieved in spirit,
Even like a wife of one's youth when she is
   rejected,''
Says your God (NASB).

"Mary, do you understand what that means? It means that *God* is the One who really loves you. He's the only One who is *capable* of totally loving you. He's known you since before you were born. He remembers every day of your life. He knows what makes you happy. He knows what touches your heart. He understands the little things that give you joy, things you could never explain to another human being. And He has said that He is your husband!''

There was silence while Mary responded.

Sharon answered once more. "Of course you're married to Doug in the flesh. You've made a commitment to that marriage. And our earthly marriages carry responsibilities with them—responsibilities, pleasures, and problems.

"But if the Lord is really your Husband, you don't have to look to Doug for fulfillment. He can't possibly meet all your needs anyway, whether he's a Christian or not. Even today, as good a husband as he is, Raul can't meet all my needs. Only God can do that. And Mary, I'll tell you from experience—He will!''

After their conversation was over, Sharon looked at me and laughed. "Did what I said surprise you?''

"Well, I've never heard you say it before, but it's all

true. As much as I'd like to, I know I can't be everything to you a husband should be."

"No one on earth could, Raul. I really began to realize that after you came to the Lord. Before you were saved, I used to feel like I had lost you to the world. If you weren't out with the guys, you were at kung fu. And if you weren't doing that, you were surfing. It was always something.

"But then, after you asked the Lord into your life, I had a real shock. I found myself thinking, 'Now I've lost him to Jesus!' Either way, you weren't there when I thought you should be."

"I'm sorry, Sharon. . ." Her words saddened me, but she quickly went on.

"No, you shouldn't be sorry. God showed me something that took all that pain away. One night I was outside, talking to Him. It was a clear, moonless night, and it seemed like I could see every star He had ever created. All of a sudden a shooting star darted across the sky and disappeared. At that very moment God spoke to my spirit: 'Sharon, human passion is like that shooting star. It's brilliant and exciting for the moment, but before long it vanishes into a beautiful memory, often leaving you empty.'

"Then He showed me the rest of the nighttime sky—the galaxies, the planets, the constant procession of constellations that have shined above the earth for thousands of years. 'Your times with me are like the heavens, Sharon. I am always there. I am unchanging. I am with you forever.' "

All through the day I thought about what Sharon had said. What tremendous freedom that truth gave me as a husband! I was responsible before God to follow the guidelines for husbands that are spelled out in the Scriptures. And I will have to answer to Him someday if

I don't. But I wasn't responsible for Sharon's happiness; only God could provide her with that.

The Christian life is a solitary pilgrimage, I thought to myself. *People sometimes worship together. We sometimes fellowship together as brothers and sisters in the body of Christ. We sometimes have close, intimate times together as husbands and wives, as parents and children, as special personal friends. But my walk with God is the most important relationship I will ever know. It has to be one-on-one—just Him and me. He wants me to love Him with all my heart, all my soul, all my mind, and all my strength. And there's no way I can allow any other person on this earth to take His place.*

The next morning Sharon and I decided to have breakfast together. The busier I got, the less time we had to enjoy each other's company. We were learning that sometimes we had to make time for conversation. Otherwise we found ourselves drifting in different directions like a couple of casual acquaintances who shared the same house. Besides, our recent conversations had made me want to hear more from Sharon. It was exciting to learn how God had been at work in her life.

We talked about her phone call from Mary. I had known before that Mary and Doug had marital problems, but I didn't realize that Sharon had been talking to her for months. "I don't ever remember hearing you counseling another person the way you did Mary. You did a super job of directing her into the Word. And you really used your own hurts to help heal hers. It blew me away!"

"You know, Raul, people are always telling me what a fantastic person I was for putting up with you all those years..." We both started laughing. We couldn't help it. "But the fact is, even though I was always reading the Bible and praying, I was completely wrapped up in myself. I was using God to solve my problems, not really trying to serve Him."

I interrupted. "But you were always a fantastic wife and mother. And you never bugged me about going to church, or tried to make me become a Christian. That's one thing...you'd stay home with me and miss church before you'd shove it in my face. You were really sensitive about that. I felt like the kids and I came first, no matter what."

"It's true that I was taking care of business, and I was determined not to let church activities come between us. But I was like Martha: instead of sitting at Jesus' feet listening to Him and loving Him, I was always in the kitchen fussing about dinner—either that or reading the Bible in my chair, praying that things would get better."

I didn't quite understand what she was getting at. "But that's what you were supposed to be doing, Sharon."

"Yes, but I was supposed to be doing more. And you're the one that showed me, Raul."

"What do you mean?"

"After you became a Christian, your whole life was immediately and totally committed to God. You were willing to do anything, go anywhere, talk to anybody. You studied the Word night and day, but not just for yourself. You were driven to go out and share with others. Remember, almost the first thing you did was go back to Baldwin Park High School and witness to the kids there."

"I just couldn't keep my mouth shut. But that's the way I am, Sharon. You're more inward than I am."

"That's true. But that doesn't mean it's right to be self-centered. I realized as I watched you grow that I was like a stagnant pool. You were growing by leaps and bounds, and the living water was flowing through you as if you were a giant pipe. I was full of facts, verses, and information. But I never passed anything on. God began to convict me about that."

"What were you holding back?"

"Myself. I didn't want to expose myself. I wanted to keep all my thoughts, feelings, and experiences private. That way no one could get close enough to hurt me. But as I watched you, I realized that to love others, you have to be vulnerable. And that means no self-protective secrecy. Look how honest Paul was about his life and his feelings. And God has used that openness of his to change people's lives for almost 2000 years."

"Well, Sharon, you know what Jesus said: 'Freely you have received, freely give.' "

"That's exactly what I saw you doing. And I had to let God change my heart so I could reach out, too. So you're right. When I take the time to talk to somebody like Mary, it's a new direction for me. But you know what? I enjoy it."

"And you know what else, Sharon?" I looked at her with deepened respect, with even more love than I'd ever felt before. "You know what else? You've got so much good stuff to say that you don't even realize it. You may have been stagnant all those years, but you were absorbing truth. You were dwelling in the Word. And now you're prepared to go out and share it with the world!"

It seemed incredible that God could have used my life to inspire Sharon. She had always been such an example of faithfulness to me. To my way of thinking, she was the perfect example of a godly wife.

Later that afternoon I found myself looking out our

kitchen window, watching the sky. A storm was supposed to begin within the next 12 hours, and the horizon was already building up into one massive bank of threatening gray clouds. I noticed how they silently moved our way, gradually increasing in number. Before long a gentle drizzle would begin. It would increase. Before daybreak tomorrow, it would become a heavy, steady downpour.

Our lives are the same way, I thought to myself. *If you look at them closely, nothing seems to be changing. Days pass and very little happens. But if you look back over a period of time, everything has been slowly, carefully transformed by the mighty hand of God.*

Here I am. I have a beautiful home. A fabulous Christian wife. Three great sons. My family has come to Jesus. My life is completely devoted to ministry. Hundreds of people have accepted the Lord through my Bible teaching. Thousands more listen to my sermons and tapes. And who am I? Nobody! Yet I have everything a man could want, and a thousand times more.

And it all happened so quietly. So gracefully. Without my manipulation. Without anyone's human striving. God did it all. What can I do in return but fall on my knees and love Him?

I remembered a verse, Colossians 2:10, that I had grown to love: "In Him you have been made complete, and He is the head over all rule and authority" (NASB).

Lord, I silently prayed, *only because of You have I made it this far. And if You don't come back first, I could have as many as 30 or 40 years left. Just for the record, God, those remaining years belong to You.*

I am complete in You. You are the Head. And believe me, after everything You've done for me, I wouldn't have it any other way!